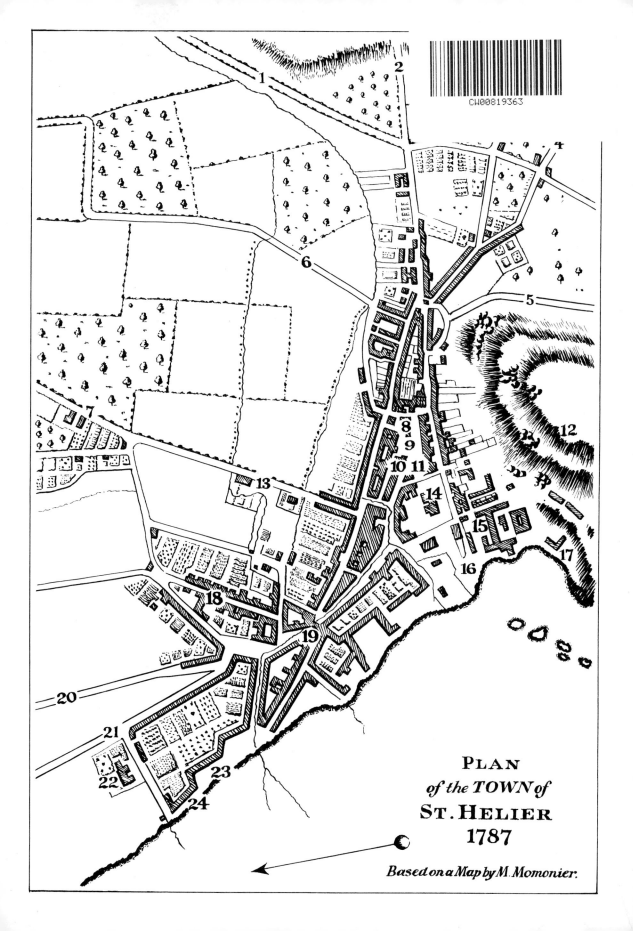

PLAN
of the TOWN *of*
ST. HELIER
1787

Based on a Map by M. Momonier.

THE BATTLE OF JERSEY

'The Death of Major Peirson at St. Helier, Jersey, 6th January 1781', painting by J. S. Copley, R.A. *Photo*: John Webb (The Tate Gallery, London).

The BATTLE of JERSEY

by

RICHARD MAYNE

PHILLIMORE

1981
Published by
PHILLIMORE & CO. LTD.
London and Chichester

Head Office: Shopwyke Hall,
Chichester, Sussex, England

ISBN 0 85033 381 4

Dedicated to the memory of
· Charles Stevens,
a scholar and a gentleman

Printed in Great Britain by
GARDEN CITY PRESS LTD.
Letchworth, Herts.

CONTENTS

LIST OF ILLUSTRATIONS

Frontis. 'The Death of Major Peirson', painted by J. S. Copley, 1781 (colour).

(Colour, between pages 52 and 53)

(Half-tone, between pages 20 and 21)

FOREWORD

Set in the context of a Europe of 1781, the Battle of Jersey was but a tiny and fairly insignificant part of the great struggle between two mighty nations, Britain and France. Nonetheless, it is a piece of history which Jerseymen recall with pride.

Frenchmen, I have no doubt, would dismiss the assault upon our shores as a mere adventure, embarked upon by a group of daring but unlucky compatriots, who were intent upon nothing more than removing a tiresome thorn in the side of France. That there was more to the attack than this will now be seen.

Jerseymen have always claimed it as a great triumph, an occasion to exult in. It was the last of innumerable attempts by France to conquer this group of islands, geographically so close to their country but, through a quirk of history, intensely loyal to the Crown of England.

Times have changed; France and Britain have become staunch allies. We have fought side by side in two of the cruellest wars the world has ever seen. Today, 200 years after the Battle of Jersey, the French invasion is one of happy holiday-makers who come to enjoy our beautiful island and historical buildings. Jersey and the United Kingdom, for their part, have joined with France to become members of the European Community: now Jerseymen and Englishmen are trying to become good Europeans.

What more propitious time could there be than 1981, the bi-centenary, to publish a history of the Battle? It is fitting too, that La Société Jersiaise should take the lead in producing this book as just one contribution to mark the anniversary. Richard Mayne's researches have unearthed a great deal of new and hitherto unpublished information which casts a rather different light on some of the events which took place on that occasion. The author, with artist Henry Fowler's excellent illustrations, has produced a book which, I suspect, is destined to become the definitive work on the Battle of Jersey.

MAURICE RICHARDSON
President, La Société Jersiaise

'At the east end of the Island there is a bay of two miles over, called Old Castle Bay; a flat fair sand ashore but shallow and full of rocks at sea, scattered here and there, and of easy access for flat-bottom boats, and where a considerable number of forces may land, without opposition from the castle or shore, especially upon a long beach called Le Banc de Vielet, which runs off into the sea, from the south point of the said Bay, for at least three miles, dry in spring tides; where upon some high sands, divided for some time from the shore, men may land and put themselves in order, before any opposition can come from the shore and the adjoining land: far from any commanding hills, being flat and champion, where an enemy may entrench.'

A Survey of ye Island of Jersey
by Philippe Dumaresq, 1685

States Loyal Address:

   'Though our language is French our swords and hearts are English.'

'Signal fires have been noted on high places in the Island, to be answered by fires in France . . . 2,000 livres reward for information leading to the arrest of these traitors . . . Notice of this to be placed in all the guard houses and Parish notice boards and rectors to publicize this from their pulpits . . .' (Actes des Etats, 15.2.1780).

'Abraham Bushell Capt. of the Privateer 'Jersey' was taken to court for having been suspected of sending letters to France to persons in authority and suspected with having correspondence with the enemies of His Majesty' (Actes des Etats, 1.7.1780).

PREFACE

Those who write of history, especially when the events took place 200 years before they were born, must necessarily depend on the writings of others. This I do unashamedly but gratefully. In this work I lean heavily on the labours of the French historian Professor Hippeau of the Faculty of Letters at Caen, whose researches in the papers of the Chateau d'Harcourt near Caen and in the Archives of Calvados are reflected in the words of Perrot, Brachet, Feron and Claretie (also consulted), which reveal so much about our island 200 years ago.

I have endeavoured to read every published work on the subject of the French attack, as well as much unpublished material found in that treasure house which is the library of La Société Jersiaise. Rare manuscripts and regimental order books were generously loaned by local residents.

The greatest difficulty has been to sift, with an open mind, the many conflicting reports, even those of eye witnesses. Tantalising questions still remain unanswered.

Personal comments have been avoided, but one is reminded of the fierce political rivalry which existed throughout this turbulent period of our history, which motivated Moise Corbet to organise and take a massive petition to the Privy Council in London on behalf of disgruntled islanders. By this action he did not make himself universally popular in an island divided by political fervour that today we should find difficult to comprehend.

Many acts of bravery that day, shown by both victors and vanquished, must surely have compensated for the treachery of others whose only motive was greed.

Now, as we welcome to our shores thousands of our French neighbours annually, it is strange to remember how their ancestors were so determined to eliminate once and for all 'This thorn in the flank of France'; the records also show that we 'Jersiais' were not quite without blame.

ACKNOWLEDGMENTS

My thanks are due to many more people than can be named here, but in particular:

Major Michael Barthorp, A. Brandon-Langley, Robin Cox, William Davies, Department of Public Works, George Drew, Henry Fowler, History Committee of La Société Jersiaise, John Jean, Dorothy Le Quesne, Ian Monins, Anita Ozouf, Peggy Poole, Douglas Shone, Leslie Sinel, Staff at La Société Jersiaise Museum, Joan Stevens M.B.E. and June Waterton.

SELECT BIBLIOGRAPHY

Ahier, J. P., *Tableaux Historiques* (Jersey, 1852).
Balleine, G. R. R., *A Biographical Dictionary of Jersey* (Staples, 1952).
Brachet, Vicomte de, *La Dernière Expédition contre Jersey* (1908).
Claretie, Jules, *Le Cabinet de Versailles* (1892).
Davies, W., *Fort Regent* (Jersey, 1971).
Falle, Philippe, *Caesarea* (Jersey, 1798).
Feron, Gustave, *Le Cabinet de Versailles et l'expédition du Baron de Rullecourt à Jersey en 1781* (Cherbourg, 1894).
Gibon, Le, Vicomte de, *Les Iles Chausey* (Coutances, 1918).
Jeune, F., *L'Histoire de la Battaille de Jersey* (Jersey, 1880).
Ouless, P. J., *The Death of Major Francis Peirson* (Jersey, 1881).
Perrot, Maurice, *La Surprise de Jersey* (1929).
Pirouet, P., *Chronique de Jersey* (Jersey, 1778).
Rochfort, Col. W. C., *The Battle of Jersey* (Jersey, 1852).
Stead, J., *A History of Jersey* (1798).
Stevens, Joan, *Victorian Voices* (Jersey, 1969).
Syvret, G., *Les Chroniques de Jersey, 1832-1838*.
Williamson, W., *Proceedings at large on the trial of Moses Corbet, taken in short-hand.* (Horse Guards, London)

Anonymous
In Peirson's Days. A novel (1902).
Relation des Attaques faits sur l'isle de Jersey (London, 1781).
Souvenir de Centenaire (Heulin and Le Feuvre, 1881).
Actes des Etats (La Société Jersiaise).
Annual Bulletins of La Société Jersiaise.
Almanacs des Chroniques de Jersey, 1854-1858-1859.

Unpublished material
Saunders, A. C., The Battle of Jersey. Notes in Société Jersiaise Library, also further MS material.
The Hemery diary. Typescript in Société Jersiaise Library. (Ref. D8 29-16)
South West Regimental Order Book, 1770-1785. MS, privately owned.
Articles in *The Jersey Evening Post*, by Philip Ahier and N. V. L. Rybot.

Chapter I

JERSEY: A THORN IN THE FLANK OF FRANCE

THE FOUNDER OF NORMANDY was Rollo. He was the architect of the settlement of the northmen in Gaul and became a Christian and the first Duke of Normandy. His son was William Longsword of Normandy, who annexed the Channel Islands in A.D. 933.

In 1066, after defeating King Harold at Hastings, William, Duke of Normandy (son of Robert the Devil), became king of England, and England and Normandy were united until 1077. When Robert, the eldest son of William I, wrested Normandy from his father part of it was acquired by William II in 1090; but in 1105, during the reign of Henry I, Normandy was reunited.

In 1204 (an important date for schoolchildren of the islands), King John lost continental Normandy owing to the defection of the Norman barons to Phillip II of France; but John managed to retain the Lordship of the Channel Islands, which then strengthened their defences because of their new and vulnerable position. The next 600 years saw Jersey often under attack, but only once occupied, culminating in the last attack by the French in 1781.

It is important to review events leading to the invasion by mentioning several of the many attempts that were actually contemplated by the French government to capture these 'troublesome islands'.

In March 1744 war was declared between England and France. Two months later two Jersey privateers went to the Chausey Islands and burnt down the recently-constructed guard-house. In the course of this year the British established themselves there. About four hundred stoneworkers were employed and granite was brought to Jersey for port and defence works. In Chausey, after the peace of 1748, the French built a temporary barracks of wood and thatch for a guard of 12 men, with an officer and a sergeant.

In 1748 the Marquis de Crenay, who lived in the Château de Montaigu near Caen, contacted the French Minister of War, d'Argenson, with a view to mounting an expedition against Jersey. De Crenay felt 'that Granville would be the most favourable port from which to embark', and another vain project followed in 1756, probably activated by the attack on Chausey. On 12 July 1756, two months after the beginning of the Seven Years' War, the forces of Admiral Howe destroyed a guard-house built on Chausey the previous year. Large French army

1

camps were built at La Hougue, Granville, Cherbourg and Valognes both for defence purposes and as a base for an eventual attack on the Channel Islands, which were a permanent thorn in the flank of France. Later, on 23 November, the Duc d'Aiguillon received detailed instructions from the Duc de Belle-Isle to organise an attack on the island from St. Malo, with about six thousand troops and cannon. Among the troops chosen were infantry regiments from Cambresis, Tournoisis and Saint Onge, as well as those from the ships at Coutances and those from Bresse, which were then garrisoned in Granville. In all there were about two thousand men.

A letter, written on 10 May 1758, from Charles Lemprière of Diélament to Daniel Messervy in Bath says '. . . our neighbours [French] continue to threaten us . . . it is being proposed in the French court that Marshal Belle-Isle lead an invasion against the island . . . I have received orders in Council to direct me make casemates in Elizabeth Castle and square redoubts in Grouville Bay'.[1]

In June 1758 the British, with 115 ships from Portsmouth carrying 15 battalions of infantry, cavalry and artillery, disembarked at Paramé. This small army attacked the walled city of St. Malo. After a siege of six days they were obliged to withdraw, but before departing they burnt and destroyed everything they could lay their hands on in St. Servan, including buildings and ships; even Cancale church was destroyed.

Some years later Monsieur de Briche, Lieutenant-General des Fermes du Roi at St. Malo, submitted to the Ministry of War a plan of operations against Jersey. As in the previous plan of 1756, de Briche chose St. Ouen's Bay as the most convenient place to disembark his force, as 'the beach is suitable with very firm sand'.

In 1771 he sent report after report to Paris. He learned that 'in Jersey were 500 Scottish Highlanders, and Invalids engaged to operate coastal artillery, assisted by 60 to 80 men of the Royal Artillery, 2,000 Militia dressed in red with white stockings, garters and cockades of black leather, black ribbon cravats and armed with a musket and bayonet'.

During this period another attack on the Channel Islands was planned by a Granville agent, who submitted plans to the French king. This was Quinette Delahogue, a ship-owner and commander of the privateer *Granville*. The Channel Islands were quite aware of many of the enemy's projects, mainly through Lieutenant-Governor Corbet's continental spies, so from March 1778 extra precautions were taken to defend their coasts, rebuild batteries, guard-houses and magazines; this work was being undertaken not only under the direction of the king's officers, but 'with assistance of intelligent persons who were supervised by officers of the Engineers'.

Since 1775 Britain had been heavily committed across the Atlantic in quelling the rebellion in the American colonies. After several cases of reversion to British arms, notably Burgoyne's surrender at Saratoga, France, Spain and Holland saw their chance to settle old scores by turning an American revolt into a world war. France sent an expeditionary force to aid the American rebels, and Britain's overstretched army and navy now found themselves fighting not only in America but in the West Indies, India, Gibraltar, the Mediterranean, and in the English Channel.

War between England and France began on 17 June 1778. Everywhere in Brittany, as in Lower Normandy, people were discussing the imminent attack on the Channel Islands. The French newspaper *Gazette des Deux Ponts* stated on 12 September 1778 that 'the British islands are the refuge of bankrupts, de-frocked monks and all sorts of vagabonds, who in peacetime live by smuggling and in wartime are dangerous pirates', and again, 15 days later: 'Jersey pirates descended on a village near Caen, stole oxen, cows and sheep, all the Curé's washing, even the two washerwomen and set fire to the Curé's house'; the local people then attacked the Jerseymen and captured some twenty of them. 'One is assured', reads a letter from Rouen to the *Gazette des Deux Ponts* on 12 September 1778, 'that ships from St. Malo and Granville will carry 10,000 men commanded by Mons. le Marquis de Castries and Mons. le Comte de Vaux to the Channel Islands'.

Some well-to-do families left Jersey because of the threat of invasion, such as the wife and children of Philippe de Carteret (1733-96), circumnavigator and rear-admiral, who in January 1781 was in the West Indies. His family went to Southampton in 1780.

An indication of the maritime strength of these islands is shown by a Memorial to the Lords Commissioners of the Treasury from Jean Dumaresq and Havilland Le Messurier in January 1785: 'These islands had at sea in 1779, 71 ships carrying 696 cannon and manned by 3,454 men . . . Not having a proper harbour for ships of war along the Normandy coast or all along the English Channel has caused the French to look upon these islands with a jealous eye . . . The fishing industry of Jersey employs at this time 2,500 men and upwards of 50 ships or vessels, in Guernsey it is at its infancy but it will grow'.[2]

Chapter II

OBSERVATIONS OF GENERAL DUMOURIEZ

GENERAL AND STATESMAN, Charles François da Périer Dumouriez (1739-1823), after a distinguished career in the French army was appointed Commandant of Cherbourg in 1778, where for 11 years he was entrusted with missions along the Channel coast and supervised the development of that important port. He was promoted Maréchal de Camp in 1788, and then as Commander-in-Chief in Belgium in 1792 he defeated the Austrians in the battle of Jemappes in November. In 1793, deserted by his troops and outlawed by the Convention, he went over to the Austrian army.

After staying in Germany and Switzerland, Dumouriez went to live in England. King Louis XVIII refused to let him return to France, and he died in Buckinghamshire in March 1823.

Dumouriez's knowledge of the Channel Islands was considerable, especially concerning the attacks of 1779 and 1781. His translated comments appeared in the Société Jersiaise *Bulletin* for 1909. The importance of his observations merits repeating them here:

JERSEY AND GUERNSEY

These two islands make the despair of France at the beginning of every war by their very active privateering, which at once proceeds to seize a large number of vessels and cut all communications and destroy all traffic between the channel ports, ere France has had time to take the necessary steps to ensure due naval protection for coasting traders. During the progress of the war this coastwise trade can only be carried on by convoys that are always hampered and often attacked and captured by guardian ships of the islands. The French can utilize for escorting these convoys only corvettes, cutters or gunboats, which lead them along from bay to bay without losing touch with the coast. Even this precaution is not enough, and if one or two frigates are added to strengthen the escort then they are promptly captured, and expose the convoy to fire and destruction, as I witnessed in 1779, when Admiral Arbuthnot burnt a convoy in the roads of Cancale, and sailed off with the escorting frigate, 'La Belle Poule'.

France can only attempt to seize these islands at the outset of a war, before they have received their armament. So soon as the measures for defence are taken, the attack becomes too difficult; the expedition would

4

cost more than it can well be worth. At least 10,000 men would be required, and men-of-war in proportion to the armed vessels which the English have in station in time of war: and that number varies unknown to the French. Cornet Castle in Guernsey and St. Helier's Castle in Jersey are almost impregnable. The French could only blockade or storm them by sea if they held the mastery of the channel. There, of course, they would have weightier operations to attend to, and would not fritter away their resources upon a couple of puny rocks.

Inured as they are to braving the dangers of the sea, the island populations are very hardy and bold, and constitute a militia of trained and disciplined good shots, who would be equal to repelling, almost unaided, an enemy that had set foot upon their soil. Their attachment to the English Crown is very strong and commensurate with their interest. Good neighbours in time of peace, having even close relations through smuggling with the natives of the Norman and Breton coasts hard by, they become most dangerous foes as soon as war breaks out. Or rather they are always in a state of war; now with the customs officers of both Kingdoms and then with the French navy. Such a population adds to the natural strength of these islands. The fortifications which, according to the map of 1783, have been erected at all landing spots in Jersey, and which, no doubt, have been augmented and perfected since, render it quite unassailable even without the naval defences always in station there.

Being Commandant (Governor) of Cherbourg, and foreseeing (already) in 1776, that England's quarrel with America, in which we have meddled only too greatly, would very soon draw us into a war, I gathered all the information I could procure respecting these two islands, and especially Jersey, which lay nearer to my post of command. I deemed it easier to reach than Guernsey, which would have entailed a combined expedition by land and sea, prepared at very great expense, and all the difficulties belonging to mixed expeditions, which always fail in France, thanks to the perpetual discord between the Royal Army and Navy.

Another inducement to simplify this expedition was secrecy, which I deemed indispensable to a happy issue, for my opinion was and still is that Jersey can only be captured at the beginning of a war, and that by surprise and a bold coup-de-main.

During the winter of 1777–9 when war was declared, I proposed to seize Jersey, by means of an expedition of 1,500 men from the Cotentin garrisons, starting from Granville. We were to leave Granville one winter's night and muster in chasse-marées at the Isles of Chausey, which afforded good anchorage. Under the escort of four gun-boats and two privateers from Granville, which were to take up a position before the castle of St. Helier, whilst 1,200 men, escorted by two gun-boats were landing at St. Clement's Bay, south-east of St. Helier, and two more gun-boats were making a feint by debarking 300 men in St. Brelade's Bay.

There were then in St. Helier's roads more than 150[1] French prizes, and in the island over 1,500 seamen prisoners belonging to the said vessels. I had arranged to take 2,000 muskets with me for arming these prisoners after liberating them, and to attach them to companies of regular infantry as these were armed, in order to prevent their yielding to the excesses of disorderly troops, whilst waiting to return to their respective ships, the rigging of which had been taken on shore. There were then in the island no regular English troops, no single battery in its place and no militia embodied.[2]

My plan for a surprise attack was adopted, but was entirely altered. Firstly, I was excluded from its performance under the very specious pretext that I was required at Cherbourg, the roadstead of which I was then fortifying as a preliminary to the commencement of the great works then still dimly projected. In vain I pointed out that this expedition, being a coup-de-main, would entail an absence of but a week or two at the outside, whether it met with success or failure. The project was given to the Prince of Nassau to carry out, whose audacity was worthy of such an enterprise. But unfortunately he was in command of a newly raised Legion, consisting of ne'er-do-wells or galley birds. It was to these that this bold attempt was entrusted, and it was looked upon merely as a filibustering raid, in which troops of the line could not be compromised, though, to be sure, there was need of order, precision and discipline if it was to meet with success. Secondly, the starting point was altered and the means of transport changed: St. Malo was decided upon and by way of escort two frigates were added under the command of Captain Champerbrand, which at once set up the customary discussions between the naval and military authorities. Thirdly, having altered the starting point they naturally shifted the place of landing, which was fixed for the great bay of St. Ouen, from whence the island would have to be crossed in the entire breadth to reach St. Helier. The legion would have got there in the greatest disorder, for not a single company of these undisciplined looters could have been kept in hand whilst passing through the well-appointed homesteads along the road.

The Prince of Nassau started under these unfavourable auspices and landed unopposed in St. Ouen's Bay, but whilst his troops were forming on the beach,[3] upon the appearance of a few natives on the neighbouring heights, the naval captain sent him a message that he could not keep his anchorage nor give him support.[4] The Prince, after much dispute between the army and navy, was compelled to re-embark and the expedition failed.

The British government dispatched a Scotch regiment to St. Helier and erected a few batteries in St. Ouen's Bay, but it took no further precautions, regarding this fruitless attempt as the last ever likely to be made. Whereupon the Prince of Nassau sold his legion to the Prince of Luxembourg, who gave the command of it to a daring and ingenious individual of the name of de Rullecourt. The latter turned his attention again to an attack upon Jersey, and adopted my discarded plan. He started with his legion from Granville and, after a delay of a couple of days at the Chausey anchorage, his rallying point, landed at night, on the eve of Twelfth Night 1781, at St. Clement with some 800 [500 *recte*] men, and marched so speedily at daybreak to St. Helier that he surprised the Lieutenant-Governor still in bed. He could have entered the castle with the fugitives, but was lost through over-confidence. The Major in command of the British regiment hastily collected it on the heights, attacked de Rullecourt, who was killed in the Market Place, and forced his troops to surrender: the Island owed its safety to this brave major, who, I think, was named Peirson. As a matter of fact, the second division of the French Legion, 700 strong [350 *recte*] under the command of a lieutenant-colonel, never landed at all, and was thus in part the cause of the loss of its colonel (de Rullecourt) and the failure of the expedition, which had had the advantage of surprise, though its preparations had lasted two months in no great secrecy.

I have cited this project only because it suited the age in which it was devised, as its execution proved. De Rullecourt would have succeeded had he been in command of a troop of regulars and possessed more experience and less confidence, and especially if he had been backed up by his Lieutenant-Colonel [Major]. Such an attempt can no longer be made nowadays. Jersey cannot be surprised, still less Guernsey. A big expedition would be necessary, and I do not credit Bonaparte with any intention to undertake it. He is reserving his great resources for England and Ireland, and it is in London or in Dublin that he flatters himself he will embody Jersey and Guernsey in his empire, by means of the treaty he will claim to dictate.

Chapter III

PLANS FOR THE INVASION OF JERSEY

MR. CLIFTON OF MANCHESTER found these original plans in the handwriting of their authors, roughly stitched together. They were passed on to Mr. Wilfred Dupré of Jersey in December 1936, and are now in private ownership in Jersey.

The Seven Years' War (1756-1763)

During the Seven Years' War the island privateers were a disastrous scourge to French commerce, and one of the best-known of their commanders was Captain Le Messurier, Commander of the *Bellona,* who was killed in battle in 1759 and whose monument is in the church of St. Peter Port. At that period the Duc d'Aiguillon was the Governor of Brittany, or 'Commandant de Bretagne' in French official parlance. In 1758 he saved his province by defeating an English invasion at St. Cas Bay. The ravages of the island privateers were a perpetual anxiety to him and he saw clearly that only the subjugation of the islands could end the peril. The earliest document in the collection (which is a plan of the forts of Jersey, dated January 1757) was evidently prepared under his direction. The project for the invasion of Jersey was dated August 1761 and was submitted to the Duc d'Aiguillon on the 18th of that month. The plan was a bad one, as its author considered that the invasion should be undertaken from St. Ouen's Bay, with sham attacks to divert the islanders' resistance at l'Ecq in the north (presumably Grève de Lecq), St. Brelade in the south, and St. Clement in the east. As General Dumouriez, Governor of Cherbourg, pointed out 40 years later, St. Ouen's Bay was quite unsuitable as the starting point of an invasion.

The main body of the troops, after gaining the heights, would march towards the Notre Dame de la Hougue (La Hougue Bie), after detaching a corps to march south-east to St. Aubin. The writer considered the main resistance would be at the height of Notre Dame de la Hougue. As regards the forts, those of St. Aubin and Mont Orgueil had their guns directed seaward and could not be expected to hold out for long, so that if the bombardment during the first day's attack did not force the garrison's surrender, preparations would have to be made to breach the walls. The project is brief and goes into no details. If the Duc d'Aiguillon did not adopt this or any other plan, the reason is simple enough. At that period there was bitter jealousy between the French army and navy and it was difficult to get the officers to take action in unison, and for a hazardous enterprise such as the conquest of the islands, such unity was indispensable.

The American War of Independence (1775–1783)

D'Aiguillon returned to Court in 1768 and had no part in the great War of American Independence, with France on the side of the rebelling colonials. With the outbreak of war the island's privateers again got busy and committed huge depradations. One ship, the *Resolution,* in 1779 captured three prizes worth 134,589 livres. The cutter and the brigs of John Tupper in the same year brought in eight prizes, valued in all at 59,374 livres; whilst in 1782 the *John Le Messurier* of Alderney, with a fleet of eight privateers, won prizes to the value of 212,381 livres. The French coastal trade could only be carried on by convoys which were, moreover, frequently attacked by the guard-ships of the islands. In 1779 Admiral Arbuthnot burned a convoy in Cancale Roads and captured a frigate called *La Belle Poule.* The problem of an invasion of the islands became a matter for urgent consideration, and the collection fortunately preserves the most important of the plans submitted to the Government.

The La Bretonnière Plan

The Naval Minister at that period was A. De Sartine, who had replaced Turgot in 1774. All the following memoirs must in consequence have been directed to him, the most important of them being that of M. de la Bretonnière, which is of great length and full of detail. The writer knew what he was discussing, but unfortunately for himself (and for us) his style was obscure and marred by constant repetitions which must have prejudiced the success of his memoir. La Bretonnière begins by contrasting the small population of England with those of France and Spain, which were then four times greater, and ascribes to England's commerce alone her strength and greatness. To conquer England it was thus essential to destroy her commerce. Now, the promptest and cheapest way of achieving this was to have a fleet of superior forces in the Channel, strong enough to make the enemy fear the risks of a general action. However difficult this may have proved in former days, it was feasible in the present campaign, with the greater part of the English forces diverted to America. The earliest part of the La Bretonnière memoirs deals with his proposals for attacks on the main ports and arsenals.

La Bretonnière begins by pointing out that since the commencement of the war, each year has seen a certain number of regular troops assembled and encamped in lower Normandy. He considers that one man-of-war, three frigates and a few corvettes, detached from the fleet for a few days, should suffice to protect the attack and the landing of troops, and to establish reciprocal communications between them and the Normandy coasts.

La Bretonnière is no believer in a surprise attack by a handful of men. He requires a carefully thought-out plan of campaign, the temporary command of the sea, and a strong expeditionary force; no night attack, but a descent in open day. The spot chosen for the landing must be swept by the fire of the man-of-war ships, and frigates, and the troops, when landed, should march forward in close order. It is essential that the first post to be occupied on the coast should be one whither the ships employed in the expedition might retire without risk, where they could remain in safety and shelter, and whence the Normandy coast could be signalled. Consequently, whilst the main attack is in St. Ouen's Bay, Bouley Bay is to be seized by the man-of-war, offering as it does the best anchorage in the island, besides being the safest to retire to and from which to receive supply boats from Normandy. A single man-of-war should suffice to attack and silence the little battery at the furthest part of the bay. Some six hundred men with sufficient artillery to safeguard them would then be landed from the 20 or 30 boats that (with two-gun shallops) had accompanied the man-of-war. In the meantime the main attack would be progressing in St. Ouen's Bay, where the greater part of the expeditionary force would be landed under the protection of the gunfire of the frigates and shallops.

Though the enemy will be in a state of uncertainty and embarrassment through the sham attack at other points, it is clear that they will divert their main resistance to the St. Ouen invasion; their chief forces being thus engaged, victuals and heavy artillery could then be landed in the night or on the morrow at Bouley Bay. The officer commanding the ships which landed the expeditionary force in St. Ouen's Bay will retain them in the bay until the troops have won a definite position in the interior of the isle. The frigates and corvettes will then escort landing boats and transports to Bouley Bay, whilst naval stations will be posted round the island.

After at least five thousand men have been landed in St. Ouen's Bay the next step must be to establish communications between this little army and the vessels in the anchorage of St. Ouen's Bay (*sic*; possibly Bouley Bay). It is to be hoped that by then the 600 men landed will have won the neighbouring heights as well as the village and church of La Trinité. The reunion of the two forces involved the winning of the whole eastern quarter of the isle. The Normandy coast can now be signalled to dispatch boats with reinforcements, which boats will return to France with prisoners and such island notables as may have been secured. The most suitable harbours in France for the assembling of such help or reinforcements are considered by La Bretonnière to be Carteret, Portbail and Pirou.

The troops' next objective must be Mont Orgueil Castle, which he considers can be easily captured. Here communications with the Normandy coast will be resumed, the signals being repeated every four hours. The artillery and munitions taken in this castle will serve for the reduction of St. Helier's Castle (Elizabeth Castle). The distance thereto is inconsiderable, and there would be no great difficulty in transporting artillery to the Pointe-des-Pas from whence the town and castle of St. Helier could be attacked. Meanwhile, in the interior, care must be taken to reassure the inhabitants and to guarantee quiet possession of their properties to all civilians who do not take up arms. Manifestos to this effect should be widely distributed. It is important, he adds, to occupy the churches, as these are the storage places for the militia field guns, while each church tower is furnished with small guns of its own, wherewith to sweep the neighbouring countryside. (There is no evidence to substantiate the latter remark.)

As the expeditionary forces advance the writer considers that the enemy troops will withdraw into that quarter of the island which includes the towns and castles of St. Helier, St. Aubin and Mont Orgueil. After the capture of the last-named, the troops will advance to the attack of St. Helier, leaving posts all along the coast to preserve communications with the ships and the coasts of Normandy. La Bretonnière does not consider that St. Helier's Castle will put up a lengthy resistance, for as soon as the Governor and officers realise that the superior French naval forces deprive them of the possibility of relief, they will put up merely sufficient fight to free themselves from reproach. The writer concludes this portion of the memoir in the following translated terms: 'Now that France is concerned with the means of protecting and the means of ensuring the liberty of her commerce, the position of the island becomes absolutely necessary and should no longer be left in doubt and it will be much easier for France than for England to preserve them, bearing their situation opposite the coasts of Normandy and Brittany in mind, which permits access on every side and with warm winds, the establishment of a closed roadstead at Cherbourg should complete the assurance of our peaceful possession, from which moment the commerce of Le Havre, St. Malo and the channel in its entirety should become much safer and would resume its normal activity when peace came.'

The next portion of the La Bretonnière memoir concerns the transport and equipment of the expeditionary force. Eight, or at the most ten, transports are to be prepared in the port of Granville, and three or four in Cherbourg. The troops in each transport must be as far as possible of the same corps, with their officers, victuals and munitions. They must be ready to embark with the least possible baggage. Each soldier need only carry one shirt in his kit bag, and other items in proportion. The naval escort will be one man-of-war, three frigates and six corvettes. The transports must be in complete readiness to set sail an hour after the embarkation of the troops. Six armed gun shallops will accompany the transports, which will have in tow 24 or 30 flat-bottomed boats. Then follow lengthy and detailed naval instructions which would take too long to narrate.

After the conquest, a decision would be taken as to the number of troops necessary for the retention of the island. Those not needed would be sent back to France as soon as possible. The inhabitants would be summoned to surrender their arms at a dépôt to be established for that purpose, a fixed amount being paid them for the same; disobedience to this order would be punished. Notice would be given as to the harbours of permitted entry. Bureaux with commandants would be established in each harbour, where the ships' captains would show their permits on arrival and receive others showing whence they came and where they were going. Any boat disembarking elsewhere than the harbours noted would be confiscated to the profit of the informer, unless a satisfactory excuse could be offered.

An Unsigned Memoir (*c.* 1780)

The next manuscript to consider is an unsigned and undated memoir entitled 'Observations on the islands of Jersey and Guernsey'. The date is about 1780, and presumably the author was a military man. It is possible that it may have been drawn up by the famous Dumouriez, whose position as Governor of Cherbourg made him keenly interested in Jersey. Dumouriez became Governor in January 1778, when, as we have already seen, in his own words, 'I gathered all the information I could procure respecting these two islands, but especially Jersey which lay nearer to my post of command'.

In his old age, when compiling his memoirs, Dumouriez wrote very highly of the Jersey Militia. 'There is a Guard corps or Island Militia which is regimented and disciplined and does services similar to those of our coastguards in France, but their reputation is better than that of ours, the greater number having seen service in privateers. This Militia Corps is about 2,000 Infantry and 200 Horse Dragoons. If one may rely on hearsay reports or actual relations, their number comes to about 3,000 armed men, distributed in different localities, for the safeguard of the isle.' Note the cautious language. In Mr. Clifton's opinion this particular memoir is one of several sent by Dumouriez himself to the Government. His own plan for the conquest of Jersey is dealt with later in the summary of the present material.

Monsieur de Briche's Observations (1778)

Our next series of observations was drawn up by M. de Briche, an official in the Fermiers-Generaux Service. It is signed and dated at St. Malo, 28 July 1778. The author gives the choice of two positions for the successful descent, the first being in St. Aubin's Bay. He suggests that a man-of-war with 60 guns should take position at a distance of four musket shots from Noirmont Point, when she would cannonade St. Aubin's Fort in front and Elizabeth Castle in the rear. The landing of the troops would be effected in flat-bottomed boats, to the right and left of the redoubt, situated in the centre of the bay and facing both forts. The alternative was in St. Brelade's Bay. He adds, however, that St. Ouen's Bay was considered the most suitable of all for descent. De Briche carefully considers the coasts, commenting on each bay or inlet, noting their advantages and disadvantages, the character of their shores, depth of water, dangers from rocks and what winds would be most favourable for landing. It is to be noted that according to M. de Briche these observations, as well as others by him on Guernsey, were collected and edited by him in respect of an order he received from the king's minister, M. de Sartine.

Juillot's letters (1778)

There now follow three interesting dispatches from Juillot, the Port Commandant of St. Malo, to M. de Sartine. His interest was mainly in Guernsey, the headquarters of the privateers which were such a curse to French shipping, but as the second dispatch, dated 22 December 1778, concerns both islands, it may be dealt with here.

He writes in urgency to point out that at that date, whether by chance or purpose, there were sufficient ships and troops at St. Malo to effect the conquest of either Jersey or Guernsey. He gives the names of the ships and puts the number of troops there at three thousand. He begs de Sartine to order the ships to remain at St. Malo on some pretext, and to hasten the reunion in that port of the Brest and Havre convoys. At the same time, instructions should be sent to the Prince du Montbarry, commanding the troops in the province, and orders (in blank) from the king should be given for the regiments concerned to march to St. Malo at a suitable moment. 'Do this, Monsieur' addes Juillot, 'and I promise you, on my honour, to embark them all the same day and to have everything ready for their departure the next morning, and their landing on the islands that same evening or the following night'.

As for the admiral in command he suggests M. de la Touce Tréville, but begs that he be sent incognito for greater secrecy. The land forces would need one general officer but no staff officers and no tents, baggage or camp followers. Juillot's enthusiasm makes him wax lyrical at the close. 'I dream', he writes, 'night and day of this project. I see on all sides many chances and few risks, and now whether by luck or aforethought, here we have all the necessary forces united and unsuspected, so that nothing should hinder us from performing a memorable exploit.'

Judging by these letters, the French postal service seems to have been extremely defective. The distance from St. Malo to Paris is not so very great, but Juillot's first letter, dated 17 November, was not received until 3 December. His second, dated 22 December, was not received until 11 January; that is to say that the post took from 16 to 20 days for a journey that would have been completed in England within three days.

Some Comments on the Papers

It may be asked why, with such valuable and correct information available, the French Government did not attempt the conquest of the islands, especially as at no period in history was there a more favourable time for an expedition than these years from 1778 to 1783, when the greater part of the English fleet was in American waters. Firstly, the jealousy between the officers of the navy and the army made it impossible for them to work harmoniously or under a single commander. This complication forces itself upon us again and again. Secondly, there were certain observed notions of honour current among the noble officers of the Ancien Régime. They resented the idea of detaching troops of the royal regiments on what they considered to be a mere filibustering expedition, and they did all they could to prevent themselves or their soldiers from being used for such a purpose. Thirdly, with one exception, there was the general incompetence of all concerned. The exception, of course, was General

Dumouriez. This able soldier submitted a plan which under his skilled command would undoubtedly have succeeded. It may be compared with those given in the manuscript.

The final piece in the collection refers to both Jersey and Guernsey and is an official document issued from the Ministry of War. It gives exhaustive details as to the number of men, horses, cannon, munitions, provisions, and so on, needed for the expedition. The number of lighters and boats required, the ports of embarkation and the most suitable spots for landing; all are covered and all are valuable enough in their place, but dull material for the reader. There are, however, two little points to be noted. The first is the absolute necessity for secrecy in the preparations. The smugglers of the French coast and the islands had close relations between themselves so that there was always danger of a leakage of information from the French side.

The second is the quaint proposal for reconnoitring the islands. Two blank passports were to be procured and the holders sent to England for the ostensible purpose of purchasing cloth, coal and tobacco. If there were difficulties with the first two items, they were allowed to purchase 1,000lbs. of tobacco, which would be bought back off them at the rate of 20 sous per pound. Under cover of these passports they were to get all the information they could about the strength of the Jersey defences.

Chapter IV

THE INVASION ATTEMPT OF 1779

FROM THE OUTBREAK OF WAR between Britain and France in June 1778, there were over a hundred demands from the French to their government to arm corsairs to protect shipping from the audacious attacks of the British navy and Channel Island privateers.

The following year it was decided to attack Jersey. The man chosen to lead the French force was Charles Henry Otto of Nassau-Siegen, the Prince of Nassau, illegitimate son of Guillaume of Nassau. Charles had sailed round the world with Bougainville, the French navigator and explorer, and with the king's blessing had raised troops from the coasts of Normandy and Brittany. These, with officers, totalled 6,000 men, and were to be escorted by six frigates and one ship mounting 64 cannon.

On 19 April 1779, 1,500 men arrived at St. Malo. Their departure for Jersey was delayed by adverse weather and they camped on the small island of Cézembre, just off St. Malo. At 6 p.m. on the 30th they embarked for Jersey with 42 (Brachet says 51) flat-bottomed boats varying from 4 to 20 tons, escorted by the king's ships *Diane, Danae, Valeur* and *l'Ecluse,* also a corvette from Granville, the *Pilote des Indes*, and a privateer, the *Duc de Montmartre*, armed with 20 cannon. Her captain was Champerbrand, who was also the flotilla commander. Their destination was St. Ouen's Bay.

It was terrible weather and during the night the rain lashed down in torrents. In the morning the wind carried them opposite St. Aubin, and at 9 a.m., after tacking against the wind for several hours in full view of the inhabitants, who lost no time in sounding the alert, they were west of St. Ouen's Bay. Major Corbet, the Lieutenant-Governor, and commander of all military forces in the island, called out the 78th Highlanders (the regular garrison), the Militia and units of the Royal Jersey Artillery.[1]

At 7 a.m., when the enemy were sighted, Corbet hurried to St. Ouen's Bay with the 78th and Militia. There he sat all day watching the absurdest of fiascos. He dated his dispatch to Lord Weymouth 'from the heights above St. Ouen's Bay . . . observing the movements of the enemy. 3 p.m.'. After the withdrawal of the French forces Corbet sat up all night in a St. Lawrence guard-house receiving hourly reports by cavalry troopers from every coast. But the French were back in St. Malo.

At St. Ouen, a grandson of one of the exiles at the time of the Edict of Nantes (1686), Jean du Parcq, took the offensive. He had served in an English regiment as chaplain in the Seven Years' War.[2] A rector and soldier, he exercised a great influence upon those who heard him. He sent for a king's gunner (probably an Invalid), an aged artilleryman named John Clerc. The two of them, aided by inhabitants of the area, collected several cannon which were kept in the parish, three of small calibre and two eight-pounders. These they got down with considerable difficulty over the dunes, pulling the guns across the sands and erecting them as a battery on the beach. On firing, one of them burst and wounded Thomas Picot of St. Peter, who later died of his wounds.[3]

With two sheep killed by French cannon, these were thought to be the only casualties of the day, yet we read in the *Actes des États* for 1780 'the request of Doctors Ferguson and Allez for a pension for the sons of Jean Kerbey, wounded on the 1st May, 1779, amounting to £159–9 shillings and 4 pence'. From the top of the cliffs the Jersey defenders deployed themselves gradually in a single rank, 400 foot soldiers and 40 mounted. It is on record (Perrot) that the French only discharged 31 cannon shots during that action. The site of the Jersey guns on that day was, at least until 1815, known as du Parcq Battery and was situated 250 yards north from what is now Kempt Tower. A permanent battery was established after the action, which by 1787 and until 1815 contained three 24-pounders on a wooden platform.

The *Gazette de L'Europe* of 7 May 1779 reported 'that the Prince actually landed with some of his troops and issued a proclamation stating that in future the island will form part of the Duchy of Normandy'.

The falling of the tide caused apprehension for the masters of the French ships as they feared losing their uninsured vessels.[4] A rising wind and stormy sea forced the first few who had intended to land to withdraw, one by one, and set sail back to France; they consoled themselves by capturing a Guernsey privateer mounting 15 cannon. They reached St. Malo by 9 p.m., and French public opinion was severe against Nassau for his failure. Reprisals were expected by the British for which the French did not have long to wait.

Meanwhile, Nassau's ships had sheltered along the French coast and he, with his troops, returned to shelter on the island of Cézembre to await a further opportunity to attack Jersey again. He was also awaiting authorisation from the French Court, which arrived on the evening of 6 May 1779; but as the boats were being prepared, a courier arrived from M. de Sartine of Versailles ordering the cancellation of the attack and the disarmament of all vessels.

While Nassau waited on the Ile de Cézembre, a British fleet sailing to America under Rear-Admiral Marriot Arbuthnot met an armed boat off the Isle of Wight sent by Jersey's Lieutenant-Governor, Moses Corbet, to Portsmouth asking for help from the Governor, Sir Thomas Pye. On hearing of the attack on Jersey, Admiral Arbuthnot immediately changed course for the island and was later joined by a further 13 ships sent from Portsmouth, a total of 23 warships of all sizes. The sight of this fleet in the Channel caused the French to think that an attack on Granville was imminent. The British fleet arrived in Bouley Bay on 11 May.

The next day, five frigates carrying between them 134 cannon detached themselves from the British fleet and sailed for St. Malo and Cancale, where the French ships had taken refuge. On sighting the enemy in the roads the British vessels opened fire and the French, whose ships were threatened by a falling tide which caused most to become grounded, were thereby shot to pieces at point-blank range. The frigate *Danae* of 34 cannon was captured; the *Valeur* of 48 cannon was burnt and lost. The States of Jersey in 1779 presented Admiral Arbuthnot with a sword to the value of 50 guineas for his part in the action (this sword is now in the Metropolitan Museum of Art).

The Prince of Nassau, with 500 men of his legion, and followed by part of the Regiment de Rousillon, hurried towards St. Malo, arriving just in time to save two of the ships. These were the *Guêpe,* a cutter of 10 cannon, and the lighter *l'Ecluse* of 20 cannon.

This abortive attempt on the island immediately caused the British Government to intensify their efforts and build further defences, including the early round towers (wrongly named martellos), many of which still survive. Extra guards were established and Jersey privateers scoured island waters.

Nassau, now much in debt to money-lenders, was forced to split up his forces; 200 of his Knights of the Legion of Nassau went to America, taking an active part in the Battle of Gloucester. The remainder of his legion the Prince divided into three parts. He kept with him his staff officers and 200 grenadiers, putting them in a garrison on the Ile Dé (*sic*). Part of his infantry, 1,300 men, was incorporated with the royal troops. The price he received earned for him a balance of 200,000 crowns. The last portion of his legion was still available and awaiting purchase, being bought eventually by the Chevalier de Luxembourg (Anne Paul Emmanuel Sigismund de Montmorency), aged 38, and a favourite of the French queen, Marie Antoinette. This army was known as the Legion of Luxembourg, and was composed of the volunteers re-bought from the Prince of Nassau, released prisoners, and many who were previously detained in the king's barracks.

Money was needed to pay this motley band, but the Chevalier de Luxembourg did not have enough, and, like Nassau, was forced to go to money-lenders. He had hoped for government support, which was not forthcoming, so he had to resign himself to the fact that he was a privateer who was to be recognised if he succeeded, but disowned if he failed.

The uniform of the volunteers of the Legion of Luxembourg was that of the old Legion of Nassau—black tricorne hats, royal blue tunics with accoutrements, facings and collar in deep red/orange, and white tunic lining and breeches; buttons were white and bore the arms of Luxembourg.

With the 700 volunteers of the Legion of Luxembourg were three companies of militia from lower Normandy and some sailors recruited on the coast. These were reinforced shortly by several hundred men from the provincial regiments of Paris and Mantes in Normandy, altogether about one thousand two hundred men.

Looking for a leader of the new expedition among the old officers of the Legion of Nassau, the Chevalier de Luxembourg found the 36-year-old Baron de Rullecourt, Philip Charles Macquart, born near Lille on 9 July 1744. His father was a secretary to the King of France, but was unable to keep his son on the straight and narrow path, and at a very early age the latter was arrested by the parliament of the province. He then fled to Spain, becoming one of the body-guards of His Catholic Majesty in a Flemish company, and in 1767 he became a Captain of Infantry. He later left for Poland and took command of the Regiment of Massalsky. After leaving Poland with a price on his head, he returned to France and served in the Regiment of the Hussars of Nassau.

During this time he had married the illegitimate daughter of the Comte d'Argenson; she lived in a convent near Tours. He got to know her with the aid of a young officer friend, and later managed to abduct the girl and marry her. Several children were born of this union.[5]

He was married on 27 July 1768, through the influence of d'Argenson. In 1779 he was in camp at St. Malo as a Lieutenant-Colonel second in command of the Legion of Nassau, and although he was unknown in the papers of this corps, there is a first lieutenant with the name of Macquart who could very well be he.

Several accounts confirm that de Rullecourt had accompanied the Prince of Nassau on his expedition against Jersey and was second in command.

*

Extracts from the *Caledonian Mercury*, Edinburgh

Wednesday, 12 July 1779

Description of the Island of Jersey

Jersey is twelve miles in length, six in breadth and about twenty-seven in circumference; it is twenty miles south by east from Guernsey, fourteen from the French coast and seventy-two from the English. It is defended by rocks and quick-sands, which render the navigation of it dangerous. On the north side the cliffs are so lofty that their tops are forty or fifty fathom perpendicular from the sea, which renders it inaccessible that way; but on the south, it is almost level with the water. The west part of island was once very good land but it is now become a desert, from the winds throwing up sand from the bottom to the top of the highest cliffs. Some places of the highest lands have fine sweet mould, while others are gritty or gravelly, rocky or stony. The lower parts have a rich, heavy, deep soil. The midland part is somewhat mountainous, but so thick planted with hedge-rows and orchards that at a distance they look like one continued forest. The valleys under the hills are finely watered with brooks, that turn forty corn-mills besides fulling-mills.

The cattle and sheep are small, but these last produce fine wool and their flesh is sweet, which is ascribed to the shortness of the grass. The horses, as in Guernsey, are only proper for the plough and cart.

Their only game is hares and rabbits: but the island produces all manner of trees, roots and herbs; as also corn, but not enough for the inhabitants, which perhaps may be owing to the great application of the people to the stocking manufacture, to the increase of trade and navigation, to the great culture of cider, and to the multiplying of hedge-rows and highways. Their fields are generally enclosed by great mounds or earth, from six to eight and ten feet high, and proportionably thick, planted with quicksets, timber trees, and many of them faced with stone.

In some years they make 24,000 hogsheads of cider, and yet they export but little, for which reason, and the cheapness of wine and brandy, they have little need for malt liquors. They manure the land with seaweed in the winter and in the summer use it for fuel, the ashes of which are very good to improve the land, for which purpose they strew it over the green sward. Though the whole island is, as it were, one entire rock, yet there is scarce a house but what has a spring bubbling near it; and one of which has a purging quality, found out by Dr. Charlton. Their butter and honey are so good, that they bear four times the price of what are brought from France.

Here are but two principle towns, St. Helier and St. Aubin. St. Helier, the capital, situated very commodiously and pleasantly in the bay of St. Aubin, having the sea on the south-west, and sheltered with hills on the north, has a stone pier and a good harbour, consists of about 400 houses, with wide streets, and well paved, and watered by a rivulet of pure water, that enters the streets and the very houses, so as to be drawn up by buckets. Here is a large square well built, in which stands the seat of justice. The town is chiefly inhabited by shop-keepers, artificers, and retailers of brandy etc. The number of inhabitants are computed at 2,000 and upwards, who want for neither the necessaries or the conveniences of life. The market is kept every Saturday and resembles a fair more than a common market, from the concourse of people that resort to it from all parts of the island. The corn market is under a piazza, and the shambles are in a spacious hall, so enclosed so as not to annoy passengers with either the sight or smell of the butchers' meat.

Here is but one church, where prayers are read in French and English alternately.

St. Aubin is the best and most frequented port in the island, neatly built in the modern taste and inhabited principally by merchants and masters, etc. of ships; but it is not above half as big as St. Helier, being straightened between the hills and the sea. The chapel in this town was built by contributions, and is a member of the church of St. Brelade. The harbour is rendered safe and quiet by a fort with cannon planted on bastions, and a pier that joins the fort and runs out into the sea, like that at Guernsey; and no ship can come into it without passing under the guns. Here a sixth-rate man of war can just float at dead neap, and a ship of 200 tons at all times. A vessel of 130 tons may come in at half flood: but larger ships and men of war must keep in the road, where there is good anchorage.

The houses in general throughout the island are built very strong with a kind of rag stone, and some of another sort from Mont-Mado-hill. Some of the best, as well as the churches, are covered with slates, but they are generally thatched.

In time of war they trade to England and Newfoundland; but in time of peace with France, Spain and Portugal. Their principal manufacture is knitting of stockings etc., in which the women and children are employed, and 8,000 pair have been brought weekly to St. Helier's market. They are allowed 2,000 ton of wool from England to support this manufacture.

The number of inhabitants are computed at 20,000 souls, whose manners are mixture of English and French; but they give the preference to the French tongue, both in the pulpit and at the bar and speak with more propriety than in any other of the southern provinces of Frances.

The militia appear in habit and discipline like regular forces. Every man in the island is exercised, disciplined and does continual duty. The better sort are their commission-officers. They consist of two troops of horse and five regiments of foot, who are reviewed every 29th May. Two or three parishes make up a regiment. There are twenty-five or more brass field pieces, mounted on carriage, with proper tumbrels for the ammunition of this militia, which pieces are kept in the parish churches they belong to, ready to be drawn out for service upon a minute's warning. Besides, there are guard-houses erected, and batteries, with about fifty eighteen-pounders, in places accessible by an enemy on the coast of this island.

The Lieutenant-Governor resides in the castle; the Governor seldom honouring the island with his company.

Extract of a letter from Moses Corbet, Esq., Lieutenant-Governor of Jersey, to the Lord Viscount Weymouth (from the *Caledonian Mercury*)

From the heights of St. Ouen's Bay, attending to the motions of the enemy: Jersey, May 1st, 1779, three o'clock in the afternoon.

Early this morning five large vessels, and a great number of boats (which afterwards appeared to be French) were seen within three leagues of the coast, from whence they proceeded to St. Ouen's Bay, in order, by a coup-de-main, to effect a landing. The cutters and small craft intended to cover their

1. 'The Battle of Jersey', painting by E. F. Burney, *c.*1787. (Société Jersiaise Museum.)

2. Major Francis Peirson.

3a & b. Major Peirson's watch. This was stolen from the Jersey Museum in 1960. (Société Jersiaise.)

Major Moise Corbet, Lieutenant-Governor.

5. Moise Corbet directing the defences against the French attack of 1779 in St. Ouen's Bay, from a painting by Philippe Jean. (Société Jersiaise Museum.)

(*opposite above*) Moise Corbet's residence, 'Maison la Motte', in the 1930s. (Société Jersiaise.)

(*opposite below*) The rear of Corbet's house, where he was arrested, at the corner of James Street and Grosvenor Street in the 1930s. The shop stands on the site of the former ballroom. (Société Jersiaise.)

8. (*above*) Baron de Rullecourt. (Société Jersiaise Museum.)

De Par Le Roy

9. (*left*) One of de Rullecourt's proclamations: note he signs himself as General. (Société Jersiaise.)

10. 'The Taking of La Rocque Battery by the 83rd Regiment and Jersey Militia', painting by P. J. Ouless.

11. *The Monsieurs Mistaken*, caricature published by E. Heayes in 1781. (Société Jersiaise Library.)

12. The 95th Regiment rushing their artillery to Mont Patibulaire.

13. The French surrender, 1781 (allegorical).

14. The tower and guard-house at La Rocque in 1781, from a painting by Alexander Shepherd M.A. (Société Jersiaise Museum.)

15. St. Helier harbour and Elizabeth Castle in 1781.

16. Fort Henry, Grouville, in 1939. (Photo: E. Guiton.)

17. Seymour Tower at low tide.

18. 'The North-East View of the Town Hill', painting by Joseph Heath, 1758. (Société Jersiaise.)

19. (*top*) The parish church of St. Helier from the south, *c.* 1920.

20. (*centre*) The parish church of Grouville.

21. (*left*) The parish church of St. Clement's.

22.   St. Helier and the Town Hill seen from Mont Patibulaire or Gallows Hill, now Westmount.

Charing Cross, Jersey.

.   Charing Cross, Jersey: the old prison stood on this site in 1781. Note Rue Derrière (King Street) on the
t and Rue d'Egypte (Broad Street) on the right.

24. Captain Clement Hemery, Royal Jersey Artillery

25. Royal Square, *c.* 1860. The house from which Hemery escaped became 'Perrot's' printers.

6. Edouard Millais as a young man (from *Life and Letters of J. E. Millais*, by J. G. Millais, 1899).

27. Le Tapon Farm, St. Saviour.

28. Peirson Place in 1836.

29. Mrs. Nicholas Fiott and the musket ball which struck her shoulder.

30. Memorial to Major Francis Peirson by Bacon in St. Helier's parish church.

31. Memorial to seven grenadiers of the 83rd Regiment.

32. Scene today, showing the statue (centre) and Ro Court (behind). The door the left roughly marks the spot where Major Peirson shot.

33. Scene today from the statue. The building on the right was Dr. Lerrier's house.

34. Scene today at the sta note the extra storey which was added to Dr. Lerrier's house.

disembarkation, came so near as to throw some grape shot, and the boats were at hand to effect their purpose; but by the spirited march of the 78th, and the militia of the island with some few of the artillery of the island, which we able to drag through the heavy sands, they were beat off, and obliged to give up their hostile intentions in that bay, without any loss on our side than a few men wounded by the bursting of a cannon; but the enemy remains within about a league of the coast, lying to, in order as we suppose, when the tide permits, to make a further attempt; in which case nothing shall be wanting on our part. The King's troops and militia have already gone through great fatigue, and show a spirit beyond my power to describe.

*

Admiralty-office, May 8th. 1779

In consequence of intelligence received last week of an attack intended to be made by the French on the islands of Jersey and Guernsey, orders were immediatly dispatched to the commanding officers of his Majesty's ships at Portsmouth and Plymouth, to send a number of frigates and sloops for the protection of those islands; since which two letters to Mr. Stephens have been received from Admiral Arbuthnot, of which the following are extracts:

Europe, at sea. May 2nd, ten o'clock, A.M.

Having this moment learnt, that the island of Jersey was yesterday morning attacked by five French ships of war, several bomb vessels, and fifty boats, which were landing men at eleven o'clock, I desire you will please acquaint their Lordships therewith, and that I think it is my duty to give every possible relief to it; for which purpose I am now shaping my course thither.

Europe, at sea. May 6th.

I omitted in my letter of the 2nd to inform their Lordships, that by the vessel dispatched, for their information, of the intelligence I had received of Jersey being attacked, I had also sent a duplicate of it to Admiral Sir Thomas Pye, who, I find by his letter which I received last night, transmitted to me by the Governor of Guernsey, was sending a very sufficient force for the security of those islands. The Lieutenant-Governor of Guernsey acquaints me that a boat from Jersey arrived at Guernsey on Sunday, and says that an armament attempted to land but could not accomplish their design; that they then stood out to sea and have returned either to St. Cas Bay or to Cape Frehel. Captain Ford of the 'Unicorn' has, in my opinion, a force under his command sufficient for the protection of those islands. I therefore leave the direction of the King's service there in his hands: and am now proceeding to Torbay, to rejoin the trade, and, in my way, expect to be joined by the 'Experiment', which I detached the evening before last to Guernsey.

House of Lords, Friday, May 7th. (From the *Caledonian Mercury*)

The Earl of Bristol informed the House that he thought it his duty to omit no opportunity of convincing their Lordships by every new argument, as it might arise, in what bad hands the directions of our naval affairs were; a circumstance had recently occurred to strengthen his former assertions on that subject. The French had embarked with a considerable squadron and made a descent upon an island, just at our elbow, which was exceedingly ill-provided for such an attack. Why had not the Ministry of the marine department a small fleet of observation, a frigate, or even a skull in the channel to bring him immediate intelligence of any operation the French fleets might appear to be meditating? This was surely a culpable omission and was a powerful confirmation of the opinions he had maintained on a late debate. . . . Another circumstance that induced him to get up was this: . . . he understood that the island of Jersey was to owe its defence to the intervention of Admiral Arbuthnot's squadron. The Admiral took this step upon himself; it was flatly repugnant to his orders and instructions. What, therefore, he now wished to hear from some ministerial authority was, whether or no they approved of what the Admiral had done; . . . they might otherwise, forming their judgement from the event endeavour to hide any misfortune that might arise in America, from the delay of the Admiral's squadron, under his disobedience, and make what was intended as a necessary deviation from orders, extorted by emergency, a subject of legal accusation and enquiry. He hoped and believed the success of the measure would be equal to the goodness of the intention that induced it, but events oftentimes depended on contingencies— contingencies were casual and a man ought not to suffer in his person or character from so vague a foundation.

He begged therefore to know the opinion of men in power beforehand. Very great ill-consequences might arise from the detention of the three hundred vessels which the Admiral was to convoy; many ill consequences might arise from the detention of the reinforcements intended for America; and that the blame imputed to such consequences might not be ascribed to his brave friend, he again solicited information in that respect, in what light his late measure had been considered.

After a variety of other mixed matter, his Lordship concluded with a sad preface to our approaching end. No motion followed this speech.

A total silence now took place, everybody expecting Lord Sandwich to rise in reply; the expectations of the House, however, were for the present disappointed, His Lordship not choosing to humour the whimsical requisitions of an individual, on subjects, in the first place, not properly before them, and in the next, founded on the insubstantial basis of mere imagination, or a premature supposition of what might be.

Lord Bristol was provoked at this taciturnity, rose again and called the silence of the First Lord of the Admiralty a contempt of the House.

Lord Sandwich, unwilling to incur such a censure, rose and explained to their Lordships the motives for his silence.

A vague charge had been laid against him for not watching the motions of the enemy and for not providing against the consequences of a French embarkation; this was a serious imputation, if properly adduced: it required a large explanation of various circumstances and was not to be answered to on the moment; let the noble Lord fix a day for the investigation of the subject, and he was ready to meet him; but he did not think it by any means a duty to enter into a serious defence, against so irregular an accusation; discoveries of circumstances and transactions were indeed at this time delicate subjects, and should be delicately handled. As for the other matter, respecting Admiral Arbuthnot, he did not think himself under any obligation to reply to that neither, for the Admiral had himself received letters on that head, which he might produce if necessary, on any future occasion. He would, however, under the inducement of civility, though not necessity, satisfy their Lordships' curiosity on this subject. Admiral Arbuthnot had received approbation for his conduct. He had written personally to praise him, and the whole board had also written collectively for the same purpose; so that the Admiral had ample security against any future attack upon his fame or person, which should originate in the Admiralty.

The Duke of Richmond observed upon this, that though he highly approved of the general character of Admiral Arbuthnot, it was a dangerous precedent for military men, under a particular command, to have an option of changing that command, because they thought other services demanded their attention. Such a conduct was ever the mark of a loose unsettled government, except Admiral Arbuthnot had orders to sail either for America, or to the defence of Jersey, upon a previous information of that island being attacked.

His Grace next spoke to the general conduct of the First Lord of the Admiralty and pointing out the imbecility of our fleets, the united powers of France and Spain, the weak and unguarded situation of Ireland and Scotland, wondered how that noble Lord could wish to stay in office when he found himself so totally unfit for it, more particularly when 38 Lords of that house, and 170 members of the other house thought so, under solemn deliberation.

*

Extracts from the *Caledonian Mercury,* Edinburgh

Saturday, 15 May 1779

To the account from the Gazette, respecting the French attempt on Jersey (see our last) it will not be improper to add the following further account of the transactions of the French before Jersey, in their attack on that island and their situation when the last advices came from thence:

On Saturday morning, the 1st May, an alarm was given from the lookout, that a large fleet was steering hither from the coast of France; as they advanced we perceived there were five frigates, four other vessels and a number of boats: They made for Owen's Bay, in order to land, and we were soon informed on what errand they came. Expresses were immediately sent by the Governor round the island to call in the Militia, and all the troops belonging to the regulars, invalids and militia were shortly assembled; the works of the forts were immediately manned and everything got ready to oppose the landing. The French immediately began to get their men into the boats and the frigates stood in as near as they could to cover their landing; but the fire from our forts was so hot, that it was almost madness to advance; they, however, still pushed on, under a heavy cannonading; some of their boats grounded and two overset; they then perceived the attempt would be attended with great slaughter, and the success very doubtful, and therefore hove out a signal for the return of the boats, and in two hours time they were all on board again. Their cannon did us no damage; all the hurt we received was from our own, one of which bursting, killed, I believe, five men and wounded several. During this engagement the Governor sent off a privateer, which was lying to the westward, with the account of the French attack, to Portsmouth, who, we have since heard, fell in with Admiral Arbuthnot, and his fleet.

The French fleet hauled off and remained standing off and on some hours, when the wind being fair they went for the coast of France, and we saw no more of them that day. A privateer was sent to look for them and they were found lying off Cape Frehel, a head-land, about four leagues to the westward of St. Maloes, waiting, as it was supposed, for reinforcements to renew the attack. On Tuesday, arrived at Guernsey Admiral Arbuthnot with eight sail of the line and some transports; the same day arrived here from Portsmouth, the 'Unicorn', 'Convert' and 'Raleigh' frigates; 'Cygnet', 'Beaver', 'Wasp' and 'Fortune' sloops of war, with the 'Leith' and 'Heart of Oak' armed ships: since we have been joined by three more frigates, and ten of our privateers are also in company with them: These the next day, sailed from hence in order to attack the French fleet, still lying off Cape Frehel, but the weather proving stormy and thick, they soon returned, and tomorrow are to renew their attack.

Advice is said to have been received this day, that a larger fleet of French frigates, with many flat-bottom boats, and an additional number of troops, to the amount of 3,000, were getting ready at St. Maloes, with intent, it is supposed, to make another attempt upon Jersey or Guernsey.

The ridiculous and feeble attempt the French have made upon the island of Jersey must be laughed at by all Europe; though probably not an act of their administration, yet it was to have been supported by the King's marine, had not things happened too critically to prevent it.

The Jersey people are so exasperated at the French's late attempt to land on that island, that they have already begun to fit out a number of more privateers than they had before, being determined not to let a French ship either get into France, or sail out, if they can avoid it.

We have advice from Torbay that the merchant fleet there consist of 344 sail, and upwards of 140 of them have from 12 to 26 guns; and that they have received orders to join the convoy as soon as the 'Lucifer' fireship appears and makes the signal. The fleet lies with their topsails loose.

It is said, that upwards of 2,400 seamen have been impressed since yesterday week at the different sea-port towns in England.

Chapter V

DE RULLECOURT'S PREPARATIONS

ON 16 DECEMBER 1780 a council of war was held between Baron de Rullecourt, the Duke of Luxembourg and M. de Virieu-Beauvoir which resulted in the formation of the small army that was to attack Jersey.

The Legion, composed mainly of dubious characters, was not yet large enough, but deserters and others arrived daily, sent from the regiments of Auvergne, Poitou, Chartres, de la Fère or from Brittany, some of whom were even refused. All these recruits were sent to Le Havre and were not allowed any communication with the regular troops. The Minister sent to the Legion deserters condemned to chains who were in the prisons of Le Havre, as well as those from prisons all over Europe.

Every day they were rigorously exercised under arms, and during this time de Rullecourt prepared details of the expedition, going secretly to Jersey as a grain-seller, studying the coast and collecting intelligence. He then left for Granville and interviewed a deserter from a British regular regiment in Jersey, who in September had joined the Duke of Berwick's regiment, then garrisoned at Granville.[1]

The point of embarkation for the attack on Jersey chosen by the Chevalier de Luxembourg was Granville, and the march decided upon was from Le Havre to Vire and thence to Granville. It was the tenant of Chausey, Jean Louis Christophe Régnier, born in 1742, who was charged with the organisation of this flotilla. He had been Concessionaire of the Island of Chausey since 1772 in place of his father, who had died in that year. Régnier was involved in the export of granite and seaweed, but above all indulged in contraband with the Channel Islands, which gave him an excellent knowledge of the inhabitants, local waters and defences.

It has been suggested by some French authors that Régnier was a spy and, indeed, a very good one for France, but he was also suspected of spying for England. Régnier's rôle was complex. Not only did he take on the responsibility of finding and uniting at the right moment all the necessary vessels for the expedition against Jersey, but he also had to obtain at the best prices all the food and various utensils which the Baron needed. The secret and daily commerce between Chausey, St. Malo, Granville and the Channel Islands (of which, as has already been stated, he seemed to be a mainspring) put Régnier in touch with

26

many owners of fishing vessels. He also knew most of the pilots from Granville and the district, and he employed them to guide this little flotilla to Jersey; the well-known Scottish voyager, John Paul Jones, would take command.[2] Jones was employed by the Americans, and went to France, where he was well received; and without any government assistance he undertook a deadly and running war against English shipping in the Channel with only an 18-cannon brig.

Among the many who helped de Rullecourt with money[3] was Quinette de la Hougue, himself the author of a plan against Jersey. He provided important subsidies, doubtless a substantial part of that advanced by Régnier, which he later demanded from the Prince of Luxembourg without getting reimbursed. The 30 assembled vessels did not all belong to the port of Granville; they came from St. Malo, Cancale, Courseulles, and even de la Hougue and Dieppe. To these must be added the king's vessels, the lugger *Le Renard,* commanded by Lieutenant Pierre Ganne, the sloop *l'Oiseau,* by Captain Pétrel, and *La Petite Guêpe,* by Captain Jean François Manac, the last two coming from St. Malo. The Baron de Rullecourt had given Régnier the necessary instructions before 1 November 1780, 'hoping that he will receive the money, he will proceed with the necessary arrangements and he will be well paid, perhaps by me and perhaps by the Chevalier de Luxembourg . . . Régnier will proceed to make his preparations on the site and will employ pilots whom he considers suitable to conduct the boats to Jersey . . . and assure the said Captain Régnier that if the pilots he has chosen are able to guide the boats containing my troops, without damage, to some spot in Jersey where I can be landed that, whether I succeed in capturing the island or not, he will be paid a hundred thousand crowns, and the pilots well rewarded'. De Rullecourt did not wait for the preparations to be completed before leaving Granville. He was in a hurry to rejoin his troops at Le Havre, where the Chevalier de Luxembourg was to arrive secretly on Thursday, 14 December in order to give him his last instructions, review the Legion and hasten their departure.

After Le Chevalier du Tertre, Chief Officer commanding at the War Office, had, at de Rullecourt's express request, inspected them, he took command of this force, which was composed of 1 major, 9 captains, 18 lieutenants or sub-lieutenants, 2 aides-de-camp, 2 under-aides-de-camp and 950 men. They left the Citadel at Le Havre for Dives on 19 December 1780. The royal instructions which had been given to them demanded only that they be given lodgings, with 'no carriages, no saddle horses, unless they paid, from time to time to he who supplied them before their departure' and 'they must live by paying their way'. Also, the officers received very strict instructions to take all necessary precautions to maintain complete order and discipline during the journey, pointing out to them that they would be responsible for any damage or ill behaviour committed.

It was not surprising that such measure should be taken against the Legion de Luxembourg, as it carried with it the worst possible reputation, which was unfortunately justified. M. de Mortreux, sub-delegate of Vire, wrote to M. Guiard at Caen saying 'that every day he heard new stories; all along their route they stole and killed turkeys and poultry, and that they took from the houses ham, sausages, even a live sheep or pig'.

The superintendent at Caen, Esmangard, showed great concern at the prospect of de Rullecourt's soldiers staying at Granville. 'The make up of this force of volunteers calls for the greatest precautions, and if they were not confined to a barracks or with a citadel no citizen would be safe or have peace of mind and the public would be, without doubt, much troubled. The behaviour of this ill disciplined troop everywhere that they have passed in the district under my command, and their outrages, make me wish that they will leave my department'.

However, some old officers said to have been recruited in Germany, and several young men of good family accompanied the 'Conquering Column', and those who looked less for profit than for the glory of success, which they felt was assured, started off full of enthusiasm. One sees proof of this in a letter from M. le Comte de Boislandry, a captain in the Luxembourg regiment, written to an unnamed recipient: 'At Le Havre this 19th December, one hour before embarkation, I had hoped, Monsieur, to send you the portrait of a handsome volunteer, but the Baron forestalled me by himself sending you this present. Put it on sentry duty in one of your rooms; seeing it your friends will see that you are fond of us and I assure you that we reciprocate this feeling. I have it in mind to offer you something which will be just as acceptable to you as the portrait of a volunteer—it is the historical account of the campaign that we are about to begin and I shall have the honour to present it to you myself, if the cannon shot will permit me this honour'. (De Boislandry was taken prisoner in the attack on Jersey.)

In order to cross the Seine and get to Honfleur, the volunteers embarked in some large flat boats used for the unloading of vessels, which Jean Louis Roche Mistral, the Commissioner General of the Navy in Normandy, had requisitioned.

The Chevalier de Luxembourg often sent considerable sums of money or paid drafts issued by de Rullecourt. On one occasion it was 9,000 livres, borrowed at Le Havre from M. de Serilly, and another time two drafts from Granville of 12,000 and 8,000 livres. In a letter which du Fresnoy, a Paris lawyer, wrote to his wife, he mentioned 16,500 livres which he had had to pay on the signature of the Baron, and he added 'I have not slept for two days; when I am not working I am always thinking of Jersey and if all the batteries of the different forts were pointing at me, I could not feel more alarmed'.

Shortage of money even caused de Rullecourt to turn to his officers' pockets, and M. le Comte de Boislandry, whose credit was better than that of his colonel, endorsed two bills totalling 3,700 livres from M. de. Boulogne at Le Havre 'for the account of M. de Luxembourg and for the needs of the Regiment'. The penury was such that several legionaries who fell ill before the departure were forced to remain at Le Havre and had to be put in a charity hospital by

M. de Momberg, the mayor, at a cost of 20 sous per day, as their colonel had left them abandoned without resources and without the wherewithal to obtain shoes. One does not know what sort of reception the legion received when it got to Honfleur, but one may suppose that at the least it was cold. The mere announcement of their arrival had distressed M. de Buffevent, Colonel of the Garrison. 'As I am instructed, and cannot doubt, that we have seven deserters in this regiment, it is possible that we shall see them disembarking beneath our eyes, and that the Commander of this troop is retaining them by force . . .'. He asked what action he was supposed to take.

The Legion's next destination was Caen, where six men were still in hospital without clothing; they then went to Villars, Bocage and Vire, where they arrived on 23 December. Despite the fact that their stay was very short, as they left again the next morning, at Vire (as elsewhere) the Luxembourg soldiers made a deplorable impression. Although it is not surprising that these troops, weakened by vice and privations, were suffering from frequent outbreaks of fever, it is hard to understand the casual manner in which the sick men were abandoned by their comrades. On one occasion during the night that they were to leave, they even went to the hospital to take away the sick men's clothing; six at least had been deprived of their hats and suits, so that they only had a shirt, trousers and shoes.

Other individuals were treated no better. As they left without paying for the saddle or draught-horses which they took, the officer in command of the rear-guard refused to make payment and sent the discontented supplier to Villedieu to find the Legion. There they threatened to send him to Granville, guarded by four fusiliers, whereupon he reduced to a quarter the price quoted. All the waggoners complained of the excesses and ill treatment to which they were subjected on the way.

The sub-delegate at Vire had them supervised during their march by mounted police, whose duty extended the whole night long, and he recommended that the same precautions be taken at Villedieu, but also said that 'one could not be everywhere and these soldiers wandered in every direction and it is said that their own officers are afraid of them'.

The roads were terrible, rutted by the rains, muddy and with huge potholes. The Legion, augmented by 80 sailors and four guns with carriages, made its way slowly towards Granville, which, according to M. de Luxembourg, they were to reach before Christmas. De Rullecourt left in advance and instructed Régnier to arm the boats and to see the necessary provisions embarked. The Legion arrived the next day, the 27th, between midday and 2 o'clock; but as the Commanding Officer of the Duke of Berwick's Regiment, Ryan, did not want his men to be too close to these recruits, whom he would not accept in his regiment, they were not allowed to cross the town. They were conducted straight to the harbour, embarked according to their numbers on 25 boats of all sizes, and the small convoy left at about 5 o'clock in the evening.

Three companies of militia from lower Normandy and some sailors recruited on the coast accompanied them. A little later they were reinforced by several hundred men from the provincial regiments of Mantes and Paris, and altogether numbered about one thousand two hundred men.

With this bedraggled and motley collection, plus the four borrowed cannon and two mortars, de Rullecourt set out on an expedition for which Marshal de Broglie, to whom the command had previously been offered, had demanded 15,000 men and vessels, 'so as not to make sacrifices with no good purpose'.

The public had little confidence in the success of the expedition. 'The general opinion here in Paris is that M. de Rullecourt will himself be taken by the English and one does not feel that this loss would be very important, nor worthy of the attention it is commanding', wrote the Marquis de Lambert.

At Granville people were most concerned about the conditions of the embarkation, as it was realised that the provisions taken were insufficient. Eustache, a Granville official, wrote: 'As M. le Baron has placed all his confidence here for the poor preparations of this expedition, which he approves, and of which he will hear no criticism, I wash my hands of the result'. The result was to prove that all these fears were justified.

M. le Tourneur, the ex-mayor of Granville who commanded the corvette *Pilote des Indes,* which belonged to the port of Granville, kept an hour-to-hour account of the events which unfolded themselves before his eyes, and it may be interesting to quote him from time to time.

Having heard of the expedition that was being prepared, M. le Tourneur went to de Cerdon, the Commissaire aux Classes, on 26 December and offered himself and his services to escort the boats. Régnier happened to be there and refused his offer, only asking him to scour the sea between the French coast and Jersey to see if there was anything suspicious and to find out whether de Rullecourt's troops would be able to land without danger. During this inspection he met the king's sloop *Folkestone,* commanded by Capitaine le Peltier, which Guillot, Commissioner of the Navy at St. Malo, had sent to support de Rullecourt if he was in need of help; this was in spite of the French government's declaration that it had no part in the expedition. We shall find further proof of this official but undeclared support. They both anchored at Le Roc de Granville and Lieutenant Vallée, whom le Tourneur sent to collect information, came back during the night and accounced that the embarkation was postponed because of bad weather.

The next day, 27 December 1780, the *Pilote des Indes* cruised about near Cancale and was rejoined by the lugger *Renard,* whose commander, Lieutenant Pierre Ganne, brought a letter from the Naval Commissioner, Eustache. In it he pressed le Tourneur to continue his watch, and to return that evening to the same anchorage as the night before to protect de Rullecourt's fleet, both in going to and returning from Jersey, because, he added, the 'Court is very interested in this enterprise'. As he approached Le Roc at nightfall he found the whole collection of the expedition's boats at anchor. The Baron was on board the corvette having a council of war with the pilots, the major of the Legion of Luxembourg and the captain of the *Folkestone.* Because of the tide it was decided not to set sail until the next day at 7 o'clock, and a warning cannon was to be fired by le Tourneur, who, as he thought that he was to take part in the expedition, had no pilot. He was also short of many men who were confined because of illness, or had deserted. He asked Eustache to give him 15 men to make up his crew, and a pilot. Eustache replied verbally that 'as Jersey must be taken by surprise they had no need of him, and that his duty was only to protect the fleet as near to the island as possible, but to do nothing more than that'.

On 27 December 1780, in Granville, Baron de Rullecourt signed a very important document which tells us in great detail about the flotilla which was intended to invade Jersey. The leading vessels were to be :

Le Petit Nassau (No. 47). Capt. François Tenerie carrying Col. de Rullecourt, Major d'Herville, 20 sailors, fascines, axes, slow-burning matches, supplies for the officers and 2 guides.

Le Resolu (No. 1). Capt. François Dubreuil carrying dragoons, half a company of infantry commanded by Fraguet, 10 sailors, 10 saddles, 10 bridles, 1 guide.

La Marie (No. 34). Capt. François Les Dos carrying half a company of grenadiers commanded by d'Aubry, 10 sailors, the guide Les Dos, 4 ladders, 6 axes and wire cutters.

L'Alexis (No. 16). Capt. Giles Le Mort carrying half a company of grenadiers commanded by des Varannes, 10 sailors, 4 ladders, 6 axes.

Le Joyeux (No. 35). Capt. Giles Gaillard carrying half a company of grenadiers commanded by de Boislandry, 10 sailors, 2 ladders, 6 axes, 2 fascines.

Canet (No. 25). Capt. Jean Fuel, carrying half a company of grenadiers commanded by de Montardat, 10 sailors, 2 ladders, 2 fascines, 6 slow-burning matches.

St. Antoine (No. 41). Capt. Claude Gallet carrying half a company of pioneers armed with mattocks, spades and axes.

Le Guillaume (No. 42). Capt. Saint-Marie carrying half a company of pioneers armed with mattocks, spades and axes.

The rest of the vessels were grouped in three divisions as follows:

First Division—Red Flame

Marie de Grâce (No. 6). Capt. François Le Noir carrying 2 companies of infantry commanded by d'Aubry, 2 fascines, 6 slow-burning matches, 6 axes, 2 ladders.

Le St. André (No. 7). Capt André Marie carrying 3 companies of infantry commanded by d'Aubry, 10 sailors, and a guide and pilot, Pierre Abraham.

Le Francis Marie (No. 20). Capt. Gilles Le Tellier carrying 2 companies of infantry commanded by des Varannes, 10 sailors, 2 ladders, 2 fascines, and 6 slow-burning matches.

Le Nicollas (No. 21). Capt. Jean Garron, carrying 3 companies of infantry commanded by des Varannes, 6 axes, and Francis Abraham as pilot and guide.

Le Clement (No. 36). Capt. Jean Geffray, carrying 2 companies of infantry commanded by Boislandry, 10 sailors, 2 ladders, 2 fascines.

Le Nicollas (No. 37—the second vessel with this name). Capt. Laurent Gaudoin carrying 3 platoons commanded by Boislandry, 6 large forks and 6 axes.

L'Union (No. 30). Capt. Germain Cousin carrying 2 platoons commanded by Mortardat, 10 sailors, 2 ladders and 2 fascines.

Saint Claire (No. 5). Capt. Germain Marie carrying 3 platoons commanded by Montardat, 6 slow-burning matches, and 6 axes.

Second Division—Yellow Flame

La Malouine (No. 32). Capt. Jean Nicolle (senior), carrying baggage, hospital, surgeons, commanded by Capt. de Bétancourt, 2 ladders, 2 fascines, 10 forks, 10 axes, and Giles Perie as pilot and guide.

L'Esperance (No. 31). Capt. Jean Ameline, carrying 3 platoons commanded by de Josset, 2 ladders, 10 forks, 10 axes, 10 slow-burning matches, and Gilles Touloige as pilot and guide.

Le Père Joseph (No. 39). Capt. Joseph Fiotin, carrying 2 platoons of dragoons, 2 fascines, 6 slow-burning matches, and 2 axes.

Third Division—Black Flame

La Fortune (No. 2). Capt. Nicolas Le Mussé, carrying food supplies, and Julien Noel as pilot and guide.

Prudente (No. 3). Capt. Pierre Bouret dit la Rivière carrying artillery cannon, gunners, and François Benois as guide and pilot.

L'Oiseau (No. 43). Capt. Pétrel, carrying Le Chevalier d'Herbouville, the mortars, blunderbusses, 20 axes, 20 spades, 20 pickaxes, and François Duval as pilot and guide.

Le Saint-Jean (No. 4). Capt. Martin, carrying powder, chests and ladders. Duval was pilot.

Le Prudent Daniel (No. 46). Capt. Joseph Etasse, carrying 2 platoons commanded by d'Herbouville.

La Vengeance (No. 9). Capt. Martin Pelier, carrying 1 platoon commanded by d'Herbouville.

The above vessels were accompanied by the king's ships, as follows:

Pilote des Indes (corvette). Capt. le Tourneur.

Renard (lugger). Capt. Lieut. Pierre Ganne.

Folkestone (sloop). Capt. le Peltier.

Serin (corvette). Capt. Cornique.

As had been arranged, de Rullecourt left in the morning without difficulty and all the boats had hoisted their sails by about 9 o'clock.

Eustache tried to arrange things as well as he could but he encountered 'more contrariness from the sailors employed in this expedition than one can believe'.

While the fleet clinging to the coast set sail for Régneville and Pirou to collect two dilatory shallops, the *Marie* and the *Bon Moment,* Le Tourneur went to Chausey and put Lieutenant Vallée as an observer on one of the islets, Les Trois Hugenans, providing him with a telescope with which to watch Jersey. The whole day was given over to an inspection of the boats undertaken by Le Tourneur and Régnier.

As evening fell the *Pilote des Indes* and the *Folkestone* tried in vain to join their comrades. The wind had fallen and they could get no nearer than half a mile from the soldiers, whose conversation and songs could be heard.

A coastguard, M. de Graffeton, came from de Rullecourt and told Le Tourneur that he had to put himself at the head of the convoy during the night and that Captain Le Pelier would be at the rear.

On Friday, the 29th, the wind, fog and rain made navigation difficult. It was impossible to think of going to Jersey that day; and de Rullecourt did not want to go back to Granville, as suggested by some of his pilots. He was on board the sloop *l'Oiseau* from St. Malo, commanded by Captain Pétrel, and in a letter written to an unknown recipient he gave details of the situation. 'Send me', he said, 'as many provisions as you can. As we have no saucepans I must ask you to cook the meat on land. We have no news of the vessel with our crew, we hope to find it at Chausey. Some of our boats have stayed behind as the crews are drunkards, dunces or cowards. if you have re-captured some sailors, send them to us, as we need them'.

The next day de Rullecourt sent Régnier ashore to collect fugitives. He found two boats, one of which he forced to raise its anchor by firing cannon at it, issuing express orders for the men on board to rejoin the army. The entire crew of the other boat had disappeared.

Régnier returned to Granville during the night to replace the missing crew. 'Everyone was asleep; after visiting many beds, we succeeded in collecting a new crew . . . all the soldiers of the guard helped us to get this boat afloat again.' He then rejoined the expedition to Chausey. In another letter to the Prince of Luxembourg, de Rullecourt wrote: 'We are suffering considerably from hunger and thirst, as you did not give us any water, also from the cold and sea-sickness'. He demanded that aid be sent to him in Jersey, or at least to Chausey, because, he added, 'I am determined on pain of death not to give up except in one of these two places. The despair in which I find myself at being so crossed removes none of my conviction and I have decided to succeed or perish'.

They did not at once proceed towards Chausey. Le Tourneur saw a frigate of 40 cannon, apparently English, and to avoid it de Rullecourt's fleet sheltered that evening near Cancale. The Baron at once went ashore to see Guillot,

Commissaire of the Navy, and requested further supplies including anchors and hawsers; these he received and was instructed to fetch his water supply from the vessel *Serin*, which was at Cancale and carried 100 extra barrels of water.

On the morning of 30 December, at dawn, de Rullecourt left for Cancale with M. de Cerdon, Commissaire aux Classes, who had orders to give all possible assistance to the flotilla. At the same time Guillot sent to the boats at Cancale 60 sacks of biscuits, water, firewood and salted provisions.

M. de Castries was not satisfied with Guillot's efforts and wrote to him on 3 January '. . . M. de Rullecourt's expedition had nothing to do with the navy. It is unknown to His Majesty and his ministers, who knew nothing of it until it had begun, so you must regard it mainly as a piratical operation, in which the King is no way concerned'. This hardly accords with the assistance given by the king's vessels.

It was during the next evening that the group left Cancale Bay, escorted by the *Pilote des Indes* and the *Folkestone*, later to be joined by the *Serin*. During the night two vessels, whose crews were asleep, drifted away in the dark, but fortunately were brought back by a dinghy from the Granville corvette. De Rullecourt got to Chausey.

A thick fog enveloped the islets, hiding from view the dangerous reefs surrounding them, and the night passed without any effort being made to land. At daybreak on 31 December the Commander ordered a disembarkation on the main island, an operation which caused some damage. One boat was lost on the rocks in the harbour of Chausey, but none of those which were manned sustained damage. Four others were carried by the current and driven towards Régneville and Granville, and it was not possible to bring them back or to discover what had happened.

De Rullecourt did not intend to remain inactive for long. Having received three barges full of provisions from St. Malo sent to him by M. Garnier du Fougeray, Captain of the *Epreuvier*, he raised anchor and set sail for Jersey. The sea was rough and the winds contrary, and the king's vessels had to remain in the open sea in order to avoid being wrecked on the rocks. All the conditions were unfavourable for this operation, with which the Baron wished to begin the New Year, However, he arrived at approximately 6 p.m. about half a mile from Jersey, but again the current forced his boats back and made them return and anchor under the Tour de Chausey.

This setback could have been fatal for de Rullecourt and might have compromised his success, for it is difficult to imagine that his enemies had not been warned of his plans and that he had not taken precautions to make them abortive. However, at St. Malo it was thought that the lack of news indicated that the troops had been able to disembark; Captain Obet, who had just entered the Channel with his corvette, the *Jeune Henri*, arranged with Guillot for all the warships which were in the Cancale roads to prepare, if necessary, to sail for the island of Jersey.

De Rullecourt remained very confident, with energy that one cannot help admiring; he refused to be rebuffed and decided to attempt to achieve his aims, whatever happened. He joked about the difficulties of the landing. He did not think the British were on guard, as 'it is impossible that the enemy should suspect that the French would be at sea in such weather and at this season. They rather think we are fully occupied making presents to our mistresses, or at the Bal de l'Opéra, or as if it is forbidden by usage, which amounts to law in France, to go to war at sea in January'. He was happy that his officers thought as he did, and he said 'the courage with which they accept all their difficulties is an example so forceful, that the other ranks forget their own miseries . . . however rough the war they will make in Jersey, they can never suffer as much as they are suffering at this moment'. He ended by saying 'as long as I have one man and one lugger I give my word of honour that I shall land in Jersey'.

During four days from the 2nd to the 5th January the troops camped on the largest islet at Chausey. Historians have little to tell us about this stay. What seems to have impressed them most of all was the death of one soldier whose head was cut off by a sword blow from the Baron because he complained of the cold, and the tragic affair of another whom he tied to a rock at low tide, the rising water enveloping him, as an example to those who complained about the quality of the bread. However cruel these cold-blooded executions may seem to us today, one must remember the sort of characters with whom de Rullecourt was dealing. No amount of persuasion had any affect on these undisciplined men, many of whom had escaped from prison or from detention in their regiments; the only hope for discipline, which the situation made more and more vital, lay in their fear of a will stronger than their own.

The position of these unhappy men was indeed critical. An awful north wind became a gale and rendered any departure impossible if it was not wished to risk uselessly the lives of the men and all the equipment that they carried. Seven vessels had already disappeared in the storm in the return from Jersey, and when de Rullecourt disembarked his troops they were so exhausted by the hours of transit that he had to revive them with brandy and wine.

So it was very necessary for them to be patient and to await the goal that they could see without being able to reach. Helpless before the elements in league against him, the Baron had to content himself with camping on this island, battered ceaselessly by mountainous waves, every minute drenched with spray and torrential rain. What remained of the barracks, built a few years previously for the Commis de la Ferme Royale, provided slight shelter for the soldiers, whose time was passed in interminable drilling. It seemed that this might last for several days, as on the advice of the pilots they could not dream of taking to sea again before the next spring tide, that is to say the 10th at full moon.[4]

De Rullecourt considered and weighed all the possibilities. He wondered whether he should divide his forces and send part of them to Carteret under the Major of the Legion; according to the direction of the wind, this second section, or he, could be carried to Jersey. At times he foresaw a longer wait at Chausey than had been anticipated, so that he concerned himself with fortifying his position and establishing a camp there. His intention was that these fortifications would later serve as an intermediary post between troops on the Normandy coast and the French garrison which would be established in Jersey.

He wished at once to erect three forts: one at La Tour, in place of that which already existed (although it was almost destroyed by the British when it was quite new); another at Bretagne; and a third at Grosmont.

De Rullecourt bargained with Régnier in order to purchase his concession in the Isles of Chausey and that same day signed a deed of sale which would make him proprietor. The moment this was written, he sent Régnier to Granville to buy twenty or thirty wheelbarrows and necessary implements for the construction of three forts. This journey was the reason for Régnier's absence when the French landed in Jersey two days later, an absence which appears so curious that Régnier, in defending himself, later produced a certificate signed by a number of officers of the Legion. The storm still continued, preventing the arrival of the provisions sent from Granville by Eustache. The soldiers, demoralised by the cold, grumbled more and more. It is said that in order to encourage them de Rullecourt promised that they would be able to pillage St. Helier when they were the masters of Jersey; but it seems that he had no intention of keeping this promise, if indeed it was ever made.

The provisions sent from Granville arrived eventually but were insufficient; de Rullecourt, in spite of his protestations, could not obtain anything in that town, 'which was without resources'. He drew promissory notes on St. Malo, writing letter after letter to Guillot, the Commissioner General, to obtain 'provisions of all sorts for my troops and provisions and refreshments for the officers'. Guillot, for the sake of humanity and without orders from the Ministry, sent 'three waggons full of replacements of biscuit, salt provisions and cheese', authorising them 'to take from *le fermier du devoir* at Cancale, wine brandy and firewood'. At the same time he delivered for the officers 'an ox, some sheep and calves, which they could roast at their convenience'. Even this was not enough. The officer bringing orders from de Rullecourt also demanded ham, paté, liquor, good wine, water bottles, mess tins, and so on, and, in addition to the food, planks, nails, benches, table and tents. Guillot refused, finding these demands excessive, and saying 'these things would all go extremely quickly. And yet they all tell you that they are dying of hunger and thirst and that they are in need of everything'. He ended by asking M. de Castries, the Naval Minister, to send order as soon as possible to recall them to *terra firma*.

The thought of an abrupt recall worried the Baron as he realised that his reputation as a colonel was not sufficiently well established as yet, and he said 'there is one enemy whom I fear more than the English, the wind and the rain, and that is counter-orders and your good "friends at Court"'.[5]

The increasing requests of his men, which were also beginning to be manifested by the officers (proof of which had been shown by the demands made at St. Malo) were also worrying him. As soon as the wind improved he decided to delay no further, and on Friday, 5 January 1781, at 3 o'clock in the afternoon, de Rullecourt's ships weighed anchor with one ambition, to conquer Jersey.

A list[6] found in de Rullecourt's pocket after his death gives the names and ranks of French officers who accompanied this expedition under his leadership; the second in command was Major d'Herville (often confused with Le Chevalier d'Herbouville who was in command of the rearguard at La Rocque). Not all these officers actually disembarked. This list is as follows:

Le Chevalier d'Aubrey—Capitaine.
Le Chevalier de Varannes—Capitaine.
Le Chevalier d'Herbouville—Capitaine.
Le Chevalier de Josset—Capitaine.
de Saint-Julien—Aide-Majeur.
Baravay de Mont-July—Sous-aide Majeur.
Fournier (Capt.)—Officer de Marine.
de Saint-Ange—Lieutenant.
Le Chevalier de Saint-Sauveur—Lieutenant.
de Schacidres—Lieutenant.
de l'Ecrevisse—Sous-lieutenant.
de Gelhay—Sous-lieutenant.
Almain—Gentilhomme volontaire.
Detricand—Gentilhomme volontaire.
Larcher—Gentilhomme volontaire.
Le Chevalier de Baudras—Capitaine-aide-
majeur.
de la Gougue—Capitaine-aide-majeur.
de Bleyal—Capitaine-aide-majeur.
Le Marquis de Fraguet—Capitaine de dragons.
Le Chevalier Ferrant—Lieutenant de dragons.
Pierre Ganne—Lieutenant-de-Frégate.
de Moraval—Chirugien-majeur.
Piatte—Seconde Chirugien.

Saint-Georges de Bonnechose—Lieutenant.
Le Comte de Boislandry—Capitaine.
Le Chevalier Danès de Montardat—Capitaine.
de Stetenhoff—Lieutenant.
Le Chevalier de la Guerronière—Gentil-
homme volontaire.
Le Chevalier de Vaumagneroux—Gentil-
homme volontaire.
Porlier—Lieutenant.
Avernot de Bétancourt—Capitaine.
Emir Gouard (*sic*) Emir Said—Gentilhomme
volontaire
de Wibier—Lieutenant.
Le Chevalier Daquilhait—?
Chalous—Lieutenant.
Lorimer—Porte Drapeau.
de Lavalle—Sous-lieutenant de dragons.
Delpeche—Lieutenant.
Dessany—Sous-lieutenant.
Morel—Sous-lieutenant.
de Morainville—Sous-lieutenant.
de St. Laurent—Capitaine.
Duquerroux—Capitaine.
du Chateau—Sous-lieutenant.

Chapter VI

MILITARY FORCES IN JERSEY, 1781

THE YEAR 1781 saw Jersey as an armed camp including more than two thousand five hundred militia divided into five regiments as follows:

The 1st or North West Regiment with men of the Parishes of St. Ouen, St. John, and St. Mary.

The 2nd or North Regiment with men of St. Martin and Trinity.

The 3rd or East Regiment with men of St. Saviour, Grouville and St. Clement.

The 4th or South Regiment with men of St. Helier and St. Lawrence in two battalions.

The 5th or South West Regiment with men of St. Brelade and St. Peter.

A typical muster, in this case that of the South West Regiment, consisted of the colonel, lieutenant-colonel, major, 7 captains, 11 lieutenants, 4 ensigns, 1 quartermaster, 48 grenadiers, N.C.O.s and men, and 494 N.C.O.s and battalion men, plus 50 artillery N.C.O.s and men.

Fortresses on the island were manned by the 'Invalid' artillery, composed of aged and lame men from regiments of the British army (originating in 1688 from Pensioners of Chelsea Hospital). Under the command of Captain George Charleton a total of 48 men were stationed at Mont Orgueil and Elizabeth Castles and St. Aubin's Fort. The Junior Captain was Peter Aylward, and the Second Lieutenant was W. Crozier. The battalion company arrived from Woolwich in May 1770. The headquarters and officers' mess were at Elizabeth Castle. The Fort Major, Alexander Hogge, was a Lieutenant of the Invalids.

One barracks for a company was near what is now the *Ommaroo* hotel, Havre des Pas. Their Commander, Captain Charleton, lived in a private house in the Market Place opposite the Royal Court House.

Captain Peter Aylward was Commander of the Invalids at Elizabeth Castle in 1781. He was originally commissioned as a lieutenant in the 9th Regiment of Foot, stationed at Cork in 1753. By 1760 he was with his regiment in Florida, where in 1769 he was placed on half pay. For some years he was on half pay in the 109th Regiment of Foot until in 1779 he became Captain of an independent company of Invalids stationed the following year in Jersey, on full pay. He remained in that capacity for the rest of his life and became Senior Officer of the garrison. He was Deputy-Governor in 1790, but died away from Jersey in 1803.

It has long been the custom for the British Government to supplement the Channel Islands Militia with a garrison of regular troops to deter the many invasion plans of the French, with whom Britain was almost constantly at war throughout the 18th century. Because of the enlarged scope of the war, the British army had increased from a strength of 48,000 at the outbreak of the American Revolution to 110,000 by 1781. By the same year 31 new regiments of foot had been added to the 70 existing in 1775, excluding the Foot Guards. The number of cavalry regiments, excluding the Household troops, had grown from twenty-five to twenty-nine. There was no regular cavalry in Jersey, and the three regular infantry regiments in the island were all new ones raised during the war.

A regiment of foot had a single battalion, organised into a headquarters and 10 companies, with a total average strength of 477 men. One of the two flank companies was designated 'grenadiers', whose men, though grenades were no longer used, were picked for their height and strength; the other was 'light infantry', where men were picked for their marksmanship and agility. These two companies represented the cream of the battalion, while the remaining eight 'battalion' or 'centre' companies formed its mass and were trained to move and fight in line or column, marching, wheeling and firing to a precise cadence. A typical company comprised one captain, two subalterns, two sergeants, three corporals, a drummer and 38 privates.

A soldier's lot was indeed not a happy one. Of his eightpence per day he saw little or none in cash, as the greater part, about sixpence, was deducted for 'subsistence'. Soldiers at this period were never popular with the civilian population as their miserable existence and low pay forced them to go scavenging around the country for whatever they could pick up, to the detriment of the inhabitants.

Daily pay for the infantry of the British Army in 1776 was as follows:

Colonel—£1 4s. 0d. per day (subsistence deductible, 18s. 0d.).
Lieut.-Colonel—17s. 0d. per day (subsistence deductible, 13s. 0d.).
Major—15s. 0d. per day (subsistence deductible, 11s. 6d.).
Captain—10s. 0d. per day (subsistence deductible, 7s. 6d.).
Lieutenant—4s. 8d. per day (subsistence deductible, 3s. 6d.).
Sergeant—1s. 6d. per day (subsistence deductible, 1s. 0d.).
Corporal—1s. 0d. per day (subsistence deductible, 8d.).
Drummer—1s. 0d. per day (subsistence deductible, 8d.).
Private—8d. per day (subsistence deductible, 6d.).

The uniform and accoutrements of regulars and militia were broadly similar. The coat was of red woollen broadcloth, lined in white, and was cut away in front with long skirts or tails which were turned back to show the lining. It had narrow lapels down to the waist, a turned-down collar and round cuffs, all in the regimental facing colour, fastened with pewter buttons, the holes of which were decorated with loops of tape or lace according to the regimental pattern. This was worn over a white or buff waistcoat and a white shirt with a black leather stock round the neck.

Officers and sergeants wore scarlet coats of superior cloth, the officers having gilt or silver buttons with lace loops in the same colour, instead of the coloured tape worn by the rank and file; sergeants had plain white; light infantry companies and Highlanders wore jackets which were the same as the coats but with the tails cut off short at hip level, the former wearing red waistcoats. Officers were beginning to adopt epaulettes, but the chief distinction of commissioned rank was the crimson sash worn round the waist under the coat with a gilt or silver metal gorget suspended round the neck by a ribbon in the facing colour. Sergeants wore a red worsted sash with a central stripe in the facing colour; corporals were distinguished by white cords hanging from the right shoulder. Drummers' coats were reversed, that is to say that the coat was in the facing colour with the collar, cuffs and lapels in red; in royal regiments drummers' coats conformed to those of the battalion, but all drummers had additional lace on the seams of their coats.

Breeches were of white or buff cloth duck, canvas or leather and buttoned at the knee with white stockings below. The latter were covered by black woollen gaiters with black leather tops, which buttoned down the outside with pewter buttons and fastened below the knee with gaiters. Short calf-length gaiters, 'half-spatterdashes', were worn by the light infantry companies and increasingly by the whole battalion. Some officers wore soft black leather boots with turned-over black tops coming up to the knee. Soldiers' shoes were of black leather, fastened with rounded steel buckles and made to fit either foot. Men were advised to change their shoes over daily 'to prevent their running crooked'. Highland regiments wore the kilt and diced hose.

Head-dress was generally the black felt hat, still three-cornered but more cocked up in front, with a black cockade, and bound with white tape; officers had gold or silver lace. Grenadiers and drummers wore the black bearskin cap, which was about 12ins. high and had been introduced in 1768. It had a metal plate in front bearing the royal crest and the motto *Nec Aspera Terrent* ('difficulties do not dismay us'). The crown at the back was red with an embroidered white grenade, or a drum for drummers, and the cap was embellished with white cords and tassels. It was secured on the man's head by a thin cord passing under his back hair, which was plaited, tied with black ribbon and turned up under the cap, unlike the battallion men's straight-cut or clubbed hair. Light infantry companies wore a variety of leather caps, the most common of which had a round skull encircled with chains and a turned-up flap in front. Highlanders work a dark blue bonnet with a diced band and adorned with a number of black feathers, fastened on the left side of the band under a black cockade.

The accoutrements of the rank and file (corporals and privates) consisted of a buff leather waistbelt for suspending the bayonet and hanger and a black cartouche box, or pouch, containing 60 rounds hung from a buff leather belt over the left shoulder. The bayonet belt, hitherto worn under the coat, was increasingly being slung over the right shoulder and both belts were pipeclayed. Officers, sergeants and drummers had waist- or shoulder-belts to carry their swords. All belts in Highland regiments were of black leather.

The Royal Artillery and Royal Jersey Artillery were dressed similarly to the infantry, but their coats were blue with red facings. Their pouches were of buff leather pipeclayed white.

The chief weapon of the British Army, one which persisted in use for almost one hundred and fifty years, was the Long Land Service flintlock musket, or to quote its more familiar title, 'Brown Bess'. It had a range of 200 yards, but was only accurate from 80 to 100 yards. It was 46ins. long and was loaded by means of the soldier biting off the top of the cartridge, pouring the powder down the barrel, then ramming in the lead ball still in its paper case. This cleaned the bore and provided an airtight wad. In the 18th century infantrymen's mouths were blackened through biting off the ends of cartridges as the powder was black and stained the lips. The flank companies carried a shorter version called a fusil. Officers and sergeants carried a sword with, in addition, a half pike and a halberd respectively; in the flank companies, however, both carried the fusil. Highland officers were armed with a broadsword and dirk.

There were three British regiments represented in Jersey in 1781; the whole of the 95th Regiment and five companies each of the 83rd and 78th Regiments, the other five companies of each being in Guernsey. The veteran Colonel John Reid, then a well-known officer in the Black Watch, raised the 95th Regiment of Foot in 1780 in Yorkshire: their uniform had yellow facings. They arrived in Jersey on 13 June 1780, and camped in tents until 1 November. The Major of the regiment, Francis Peirson (1757–81), was the eldest son of Francis Peirson of Mowthorpe Grange in the East Riding of Yorkshire, who had married Sarah Codgell. He obtained a commission as ensign in the 36th Regiment of Foot, of which his cousin and godfather, Lieutenant-General Sir Richard Peirson, was colonel. Francis Peirson was then aged fifteen. Two years later he was promoted to Lieutenant, then in May 1779 he became Captain-Lieutenant in another regiment, the 75th Foot, but when a new regiment, the 95th, was being raised in August, he was appointed Major and returned to York as Chief Recruiting Officer.

In March 1780 the regiment moved to Leeds and later marched the 300 miles to Plymouth, from where it sailed to Jersey on 3 June, arriving in Jersey on the 13th. For nearly five months the regiment was under canvas until 1 November, when it moved into rented barracks owned by Nicholas Fiott at 'La Hougue' in St. Peter.[1]

On 6 January 1781, Colonel Reid and Lieutenant-Colonel Campbell were on leave, and the regiment was thus under the command of the 24-year-old Major Peirson, who was the senior officer. His immediate subordinate was the Jerseyman Captain James Corbet, son of Jersey's Lieutenant-Governor, Moses Corbet.[2] Another notable Jerseyman in the 95th Regiment was Ensign John Le Couteur (later General), who was commissioned in 1780. On leave at the time of the battle, as soon as he heard the alarm he rode to Fort Conway at Grouville and marched as a volunteer to St. Helier. Reverend Amice Bisson, rector of St. Brelade, was appointed chaplain to the 95th Regiment by Major Peirson on 7 April 1780. In the painting 'The Death of Major Francis Peirson', by John Copley, the central group is mainly composed of officers of the 95th Regiment, which was disbanded in 1783.

With half in Jersey and the other half in Guernsey, the 78th Foot was raised in Ross-shire as a regiment of Highlanders under a letter of service dated 8 June 1778 by Kenneth Mackenzie, Earl of Seaforth and head of the Clan Mackenzie. Its facings were orange. The regiment was officered chiefly by gentlemen from the sect of the 'Cabar Feidh'[3] and its ranks were filled by raw clansmen from the western Highlands and Isles, a large proportion belonging to the Sept (branch) of Macraes. This corps was at first quartered in Edinburgh, where the doings of the 'Wild Macraes' caused serious alarm to the citizens. In the *Public Advertiser* of 29 September 1778 Boswell wrote, 'The Macraes were in Edinburgh Castle when ordered to Jersey. They thought that they were going to be sold to the East India Company and they revolted and occupied a mountain called Arthur's seat for three days and nights, bidding defiance to all the forces in Scotland. At last they came down and embarked peacefully'.

The regiment arrived in the Channel Islands in November 1778 and was divided between Jersey and Guernsey. It acted with distinction on 1 May 1779 when Jersey was threatened with attack from the fleet of the Prince of Nassau in St. Ouen's Bay. A wing of the 78th, under Major Mackenzie Humberston, was particularly mentioned in the records of the Seaforth Highlanders, who were originally the 78th.

During the period of the Battle of Jersey the Commanding Officer, the Earl of Seaforth, was absent, as was the second in command, Major James Stuart. The command fell to Captain Lumsdaine as senior captain, who distinguished himself by his prompt actions. The bravery of Kenneth MacRae earned him the privilege of carrying dispatches to the War Office reporting the French defeat.

In April 1781 the regiment left the islands for Portsmouth, and in June embarked for India, when the long confinement on the ship coupled with the strange diet told cruelly on the Highlanders. Lord Seaforth died at sea before reaching St. Helena, and when the regiment reached Chingleput in April 1782 only 390 out of the 1,110 men who had embarked at Portsmouth 11 months previously were well enough to march.

After resting, the regiment took the field and served in the sieges of Cuddalore, Pallacatchery and Combatoy. After the peace of 1783 they were re-numbered as the 72nd Regiment of Foot.

Five companies of the 83rd Regiment of Foot were in Jersey and were quartered in and near the General Hospital; five were also in Guernsey in 1781. Raised as a 'Loyalty' regiment during the American War of Independence in 1778 at the cost of the Municipality of Glasgow, this regiment was better known in Jersey as the Royal Glasgow Volunteers. Despite its Scottish origins, it was dressed as English infantry and had blue facings. In 1778 some of the men of the Black Watch, or as it was then, the 42nd Regiment, mutinied on being drafted into the 83rd Regiment when told that they would no longer wear the kilt.

The Commanding Officer, Colonel George Scott, was absent on 6 January 1781, so that the command fell to Captain William Campbell (nephew of a former Lieutenant-Governor of Jersey). The five companies of the 83rd were in barracks in and near Fort Conway (later known as Fort Henry) at Grouville.

When the regiment left Jersey it subsequently went to New York and was disbanded in 1783. A small detachment of the Corps of Engineers was also based in Jersey to supervise, strengthen, and plan the building of fortifications around the island, including the round towers, many of which still survive. Captain Frederick George Mulcaster was Commander of a small detachment of engineers, and a St. Helier street was later named in his honour.

Chapter VII

ADMINISTRATION OF JERSEY IN 1781

JERSEY'S LIEUTENANT-GOVERNOR, Moise or Moses Corbet (1781–1817), was the eldest son of Moise Corbet of St. Helier and François Corbet, daughter of Jurat James Corbet. After relinquishing his position in a London legal office, his family bought him a commission in the Royal Fusiliers. Lord Bertie, the Commander of the regiment, gave evidence at Corbet's trial and spoke very highly of his military record. Corbet had served at the Relief of Minorca in 1756, and in Gibraltar in 1760, Lord Robert Bertie appointing him as his aide-de-camp. He was then promoted to major in 1761, whereupon he returned to Gibraltar and served for more than ten years with Lord Bertie to 'his entire satisfaction'.

Moses Corbet retired from the army on half pay in July 1766 and settled in Jersey. Although Jersey's Lieutenant Bailiff, Charles Lemprière, had married Corbet's cousin Elizabeth, and had also placed him in his first job, Corbet's political views clashed violently with those of his autocratic benefactor, and he became a spokesman for the anti-Lemprière party. The two factions were known as the 'Charlots' after Charles Lemprière and the 'Jeanots' ('Magots' was their derogatory nickname coined by their political adversaries) led by Jean Dumaresq, Constable of St. Peter. The island was at this period split into two determined and violent groups. Troops had to be sent to Jersey in 1769 to quell a riot and restore order. Corbet published a pamphlet entitled *Griefs de l'Isle de Jersey contenus dans une requeste presenteé à sa Majesté par Moise Corbet, Ecuyer 1770.*

This petition for political reform was supplemented with hundreds of signatures, and Corbet took it to London. Lord Albemarle, Jersey's absentee Governor, was so impressed with Corbet that he promised to appoint him Lieutenant-Governor when the troops under Colonel Bentinck were withdrawn. True to his word, Albemarle later appointed Major Moise Corbet Lieutenant-Governor of Jersey and he was sworn in on 4 April 1771.

It would appear that during the next 10 years Corbet endeavoured to improve the Militia and island fortifications, preparing for the French attack that he knew would surely come. In April 1779 he sent to England for safe keeping all the French prizes lying in St. Aubin's Bay that had been captured by Jersey privateers.

44

Less than a month later, at 7 a.m. on 1 May, the enemy was seen approaching St. Ouen's Bay. As we know, their attempt on this occasion was a fiasco and they sailed away. On 15 February 1780, Corbet informed the States of Jersey that signal fires had been observed on the north-east coast, and were answered by fires in France. These were thought to have informed the French that there were no British warships in the vicinity. The States promptly offered a reward of £2,000 (Tournois) for the capture of the signallers, but to no avail.

Corbet, to his credit, had repeatedly made requests to the British Government to provide vessels to cruise around the island to detect an invading force, but this was refused. However, the Governor, General Conway, instructed that existing fortifications were to be improved, including the round towers which are still a feature of Jersey's coastline. Moise Corbet was one of the founders of the Jersey Chamber of Commerce, as was his good friend Charles W. Le Geyt, Jersey's first official postmaster, who organised the country parishes to petition the Privy Council for political reform.

The Lieutenant-Governor's residence was then at the corner of Grosvenor and St. James streets with the rear facing Grosvenor Street. There was a large garden in front with a gate near to where St. James church is now, and the sentry box was probably here. The shop on the corner was the site of the kitchen of the house, and the two small houses on the other side of the building are on the site of a ballroom.[1]

LOCAL OFFICIALS AT THE TIME OF THE ATTACK

Governor (absentee): General Henry Seymour Conway. (In office 1772–1795.)
Lieutenant-Governor: Moise Corbet. (In office 1770–1781.)
Bailiff (absentee): Henry Frederick Lord Carteret, Baron of Hawnes. (In office 1776–1826.)
Lieutenant Bailiff: Charles Lemprière, Seigneur of Rozel. (In office 1750–1781.)
Receivers General: Jacques Pipon. (In office 1772–1814); Philippe Fall. (In office 1772–1786.)
Attorney-General: Thomas Pipon (Compiler of Code of Laws). (In office 1771–1801.)
Solicitor-General: Jean Thomas Durell.
Vicomte: Thomas Durell.

Jurats of the Royal Court

Charles Lemprière (1750–1781 Seigneur de Diélament).
Edouard Le Maistre (1764–1815 Seigneur de la Hougue Boête).
Josué Pipon (1758–1785 Seigneur de La Moye).
Philippe de Carteret (1767–1795 Seigneur de la Mont au Prêtre).
François Marett (1767–1801 Seigneur d'Avranches).
Nicholas Messervy (1771–1808 Seigneur d'Augrès).
Charles Payn (1771–1798 Seigneur des Nièmes).
David Patriarche (1771–1782 of St. Helier).
Elie Pipon (1776–1788 Seigneur de Noirmont).
Philippe Robin (1776–1821 of St. Aubin).

Jean Poingdestre (1779–1800 Seigneur d'Annville).
Edouard Ricard (1762–1782).
States Treasurer (Philippe Lerrier).
Greffier (Philippe de Carteret).
Dean (François Le Breton, Rector of St. Saviour).

Parish Constables

St. Peter—Jean Dumaresq (Magot political party leader).
St. Helier—Mathieu La Cloche.
St. Lawrence—Gédeon Dallain.
St. Martin—Nicholas Richardson.
Trinity—Josué Le Geyt.
St. Mary—Jean du Pré.
St. Saviour—Thomas Le Hardy.
St. John—Philippe Le Couteur.
Grouville—Pierre Labey.
St. Brelade—Edouard Remon.
St. Clement—Henry Touzel.
St. Ouen—Jean de Carteret.

Parish Rectors

St. Peter—Richard Le Feuvre.
St. Helier—Jean du Pré.
St. Lawrence—Edouard Bisson.
St. Martin—François Le Couteur.
Trinity—Jean La Cloche.
St. Mary—François Valpy.
Dean and Rector of St.Saviour—François le Breton.
St. John—Thomas Sivret (*sic*).
St. Brelade—Amice Bisson.
St. Clement—George Bertram.
St. Ouen—Jean du Parcq.
Grouville—Jean La Cloche.

Advocates of the Royal Court

Thomas Pipon (1765–1795).
Piere Mauger (1769–1795).
Charles Poingdestre (1772–1816).
Jean Dumaresq (1773–1801).
William Charles Lemprière (1776–1781).
Jean Poingdestre (1777–1789).
Thomas Lemprière (1780–1816).

Chapter VIII

DE RULLECOURT'S PAPERS

A COPY OF THE JOURNAL (or papers found on his body) of Baron de Rullecourt was owned by the Bailiff of Jersey, Sir Robert Pipon Marett, and was reprinted in part in *The Death of Major Peirson,* by Rev. E. le Vavasseur dit Durell, published by P. J. Ouless in 1881. The translation is worth repeating here:

There are in Grouville Bay four forts, from the old castle to the fort at La Rocque, including the old castle which is at the north end on a point at the foot of a mount. It is armed with thirty cannon, three mortars and a garrison of seventy men, officers and disabled soldiers. At the south end of the castle, at the foot, is the harbour of Gourey, used by fishermen and a few corsaires armed with six or eight perrières. Winds from the South-east and South-south-east blow right into the said harbour.

Towards the south and a third of a league away, in Les Meilles or sand dunes, is a fort [Fort Conway] with six cannon in the walls, with tiles and turfs on the parapets, so disposed that entry is by a drawbridge, the surrounding or rampart moats are always dry and never contain water. The entry or gate is on the land side. The garrison is of twenty-five men. A short distance to the west of the gate are some houses where the garrison remain in day time, there is a sentry post with a sentry.

About a quarter of a league further to the south is another platform for ten cannon. Before the war this platform had no wall; it is guarded by the inhabitants of the island.

Still further to the south is the La Rocque fort with three cannons. It is believed that this fort has been strengthened since the war. A short distance to the south of this fort is a guardhouse, the powder was kept in one of the rooms of which there are three. The powder was in the one on the westside, and the other two on the eastside served to lodge the garrison, but it is believed that the said garrison remains in the said fort as well as the powder, since it is high according to observations, it is mostly surrounded because it was formerly only a simple platform etc.

Directly below the fort to the east is a sandy beach named Croutte [*sic*] Marette, and to the south of the sandy beach is a sandbank named Le Banc Pirouët, about three feet high. To the south of the said sandbank are two rocks named Les Avarisons with other adjacent rocks which extend to the S.S.W., La Fourchée aux Beq [la Frouquie Aubert] is separated from these. There are two leagues between these where there is a small channel

47

between an islet named Conchés [or La Conchiere] and the shallows of the said La Fourchée. About the same range of a musket to the west of the islet named la Conchée there is another large rock named l'Etacheron where the said channel continues which leads to a small harbour where boats drawing five feet are able to enter.

Opposite the said harbour on the west are quite a large number of houses, but no fort; there has never been one. It is at this place that it is thought to have the landing, arriving there before low tide on a tide when it would be low water at half past midnight.

With these precautions the troops would be sheltered from the said fort at la Rocque, which is the only one to fear, unless one should have been built facing the said small channel. This is not to be assumed. However, for additional precaution the advance guard would march more to the S.W. so as to reach, without danger, the houses opposite the said harbour, and the fort at la Rocque so as to capture it if possible. Once landed the troops are to be provided with good guides in order to capture Le Mont de la Ville, etc.

Assuming favourable night conditions, headwinds from the north east, one day before the new moon, or two days after, the boats will be lead by the said small channel which leads to the houses at La Rocque.

Should the northerly wind veer to the south it will be possible to enter the said channel and instead of landing the boats there they will be led to Grouville Bay, where they will be grounded in the shelter of le Banc Pirouët about three feet high, which as explained, is near the rocks named Les Avarizons, these will provide cover for the boats and prevent them being seen from the land.

Once landed the troops will march to the S.W. and reach the above mentioned la Rocque channel. In order to place the troops under cover, the above route will not be changed by much as the range of a cannon, especially if it should have been possible to land in the said channel.

Two days before the new moon, and the day before which is proposed in the case of no moon, would provide cover while approaching the land and so ensure surprise. If, however, during the full moon good night conditions should exist with slightly warm weather, advantages should be taken of this, and it will be much more convenient to the pilots in recognising the small channel, but once again absence of moon is worth more both for safety in landing and for surprise.

Note on guides whose names have been sent:

An English soldier, deserter from the garrison of the island of Jersey arrived in France around the first day of last September and enlisted in Berois [Berwick] garrisoned at Granville.

Suspect: Mignon of Granville who has come back from Jersey since the war and has engaged in privateering with them.

Suspect: One named Louis Gallien of Bréhat, merchant, who has traded all his life in the islands of Jersey and Guernsey, being authorised by the magistrates of the places to set up a shop on his premises.

One named Pottier of Saint-Germain-sur-Ay who is garde du Pavillon of the same place.

La Cour, fencing master of Granville has conducted a school for several years and has given fencing lessons to all the notables of the island.

Good: Nicolas Bleze of Isigny has remained in the said island for three consecutive years.

Good Guides: The Clereceaux brothers of Crétivelle near Granville, gelders by profession, go to the island in connection with their business. They have an intimate knowledge of every part of the island.

Once the troops have landed a detachment must be sent to St. Sauveur to take Edouard Millais who has offered to serve as guide, and has given to the General the necessary information. For this purpose he is provided with a letter from M. de la Luzerne who was in command in Granville in 1778. It is probable that this Millais will give himself up without having to be sought.

All officers commanding the platoons are ordered to stab the first soldier who makes the least noise.

The war cry will be 'Vive le Roi et Luxembourg'. A supply of wooden pegs must be made to spike the cannons in case of need.

The junior officers of each company shall be provided with several lengths of rope with which they will bind prisoners and hostages.

SPECIAL ORDERS

Monsieur Desvaraune [des Varannes] will wait to carry out the following order from Monsieur de Majeur de Bleyal, Monsieur de Bodras [Baudraye] or myself will give the order to proceed.

As soon as he has received an order, the only one which will be verbal, he will leave in such a manner that he will not wait nor hurry. He will march straight to the fort at La Rocque, which he will pass on the sea side. He will approach as close as he can. He will use the cover of the rocks which are on the beach. He will stop his troops fifty paces from the fort and will send his lieutenant with a platoon and place himself between the fort and the houses which form the external guardhouse.

He will send by the other side of the fort by Arnots and four grenadiers with the order to seize the external sentries, bind and gag them with a handkerchief or stab them with a bayonet if they make any noise or resistance.

During this time Monsieur Desvaraune will place the ladders at the corners of the bastions, all four of which will be attacked at the same time. If there is no bastion and there, as I think, only one wall, it will be all the easier.

He will give the order to four men of whom he will be one, to be informed whether the other side of the wall has been scaled. He will desist unless he has given the order.

Monsieur Desvaraune with the men of his attack will march straight to the drawbridge which he will capture, and will order his lieutenant to march straight to the internal guardhouse.

As it is to be assumed that the garrison of the fort will not wait for the end of the scaling before escaping by the drawbridge, he will recommend to his lieutenant to be in ambush on the land side so as to prevent them from escaping, the lieutenant will leave a sergeant and ten men to guard the buildings of the external guardhouse.

He will immediately cause all the garrison to be bound and will prevent them from spiking their cannons and above all from blowing up the powder magazine which is below ground. When Monsieur Desvaraune is master of the fort he will send me a sergeant with a guide, escorted by four men, and his written report which he will pass by Saint-Clement so as to bring it to Le Mont de la Ville, where my camp will be.

If he should encounter any resistance I will send him help. As soon as the fort is captured he will put the artillery in readiness and using his sailors, capture all the munitions and will stand by ready to fire the cannon.

These notes were signed by de Rullecourt, who had obviously been given valuable information by spies or informers before the raid, indeed prior to the war which started in 17 June 1778, because in his journal he refers to the state of Jersey defences as 'before the war'. He believed that La Rocque Fort may have been strengthened, but what he did not know was that towers were being built around the island, and it seems almost certain that the tower at La Rocque (No. 1) was already built when de Rullecourt landed, although Sergeant Clement Falle and his eight men of the East Regiment of Militia were absent. Indeed, at their trial at the Royal Court they were accused of absenting themselves from 'la tour de La Rocque'. In mentioning what was Fort Conway de Rullecourt completely ignores Fort William, which bears a date stone of 1760 and had a sizeable battery in 1781. The 'platform further south with 10 cannon' referred to was Middle battery, and in 1787 it had three 24-pounders on a stone platform.

It would also appear that it was de Rullecourt's intention to capture the Mont de la Ville (now Fort Regent), though past historians have criticised his negligence in not doing so whilst he had the chance. Major Francis Peirson was not so neglectful and made possession of the town hill one of his priorities.

The reference to Edouard Millais is interesting. He was a rich farmer, landowner and shipowner, who years before had caused much trouble on Chausey, intimidating the workers and even burning down Régnier's house. Edouard Millais lived at 'Le Tapon' farm at St. Saviour, and he had several children.

Chapter IX

THE LANDING AT LA ROCQUE

THE EVENING BEFORE DEPARTURE, de Rullecourt had sent requests to the king's ships to proceed to Jersey before daybreak on the next day. They were to pretend to attack in St. Ouen's Bay, to deceive the enemy, and to occupy the latter while the main column disembarked at some other spot. The commanders were unable to execute this manoeuvre through the impossibility of meeting at the appointed hour, and later because orders came from St. Malo instructing them to limit their activity to cruising along the coast of Jersey, as close as possible, in order to observe what was happening.

It was at about 11 o'clock in the evening, on a moonless night, that the expedition arrived at Pointe la Rocque, south-east Jersey. It was a most perilous place and one which the island pilots avoided because of the rocks, such as La Grande et Petite Sambrières and La Platte Rocque, which guarded the approaches. But de Rullecourt had at his side an able pilot, born in the district, to whom all the reefs were familiar. He was Pierre Journeaux, who had fled from Jersey to France in July 1778 after killing Thomas l'Amy with his fist, and his complete knowledge of the island had led the Baron to employ him. He directed the boats, with a thousand precautions, to the Banc de Vielet, where the troops landed on a rock called L'Avaraison (the present Seymour tower was built on the site of an earlier tower). The king's ship *Renard,* which accompanied the detachment, ran aground with such force that it was seriously damaged. Its commander, Lieutenant Pierre Ganne, was able to save himself and join de Rullecourt in the forward march.

Disembarkation took place from 4 to 5 o'clock in the morning on both sides of La Platte Rocque. Monsieur d'Herville, second in command and Major of the Legion of Luxembourg, stated that 'the tide had already been falling for four hours, one of the obstacles the rear guard had to contend with was an insurmountable difficulty that the Banc de Vielet was surrounded with jagged rocks'.

One account said that at the moment of disembarkation the sloop *l'Oiseau* and the boats carrying Major d'Herville with 250 men or more, with cannon, shot, cartridges and so on was caught by the current and carried far away from the Jersey coast, and later returned to Chausey. Because of these two unfortunate incidents de Rullecourt was deprived of about 500 fighting men and only had with him about seven hundred men with whom to face the forces in the island, of whose strength he was not fully aware.

51

'At daybreak', said Le Tourneur, 'on the 7th January I pressed on towards Jersey. I saw many scattered boats which I recognised as being of our army. I pushed my way on one belonging to the Sr. Le Grand, *La Prudente,* from Granville (45 tons), commanded by Pierre Bouret dit la Rivière. I asked him when he had left Jersey and he said he had left at 11 in the morning the day before'. Some boats, having landed their troops, regained our coasts, but because they left soon after the disembarkation before dawn, and their masters had not put foot on land, they knew nothing of the situation. As for de Rullecourt, retreat, even if he had had such an idea, was not possible because most of the transport boats had left as soon as the troops were on land, and made their way to St. Malo and Granville.

Things then seemed to take on a more favourable aspect for the French, for at this point the coast was deserted. The soldiers advanced slowly, crouching down on the sand to avoid being seen, and in fact the two nearest posts were so far distant and the night so dark that the guards were unaware of anything taking place. At Platte Rocque there was a little fort armed with 'four cannon' on the way, where there was 'neither sentinel nor men to oppose them'. They proceeded without firing a shot and continued on their way across the countryside via the main St. Clement's Road, but before going further, while it was still dark, de Rullecourt stopped the column. He wished to assure himself that his instructions had been followed, that the troops had enough dowel pins to spike the cannon if necessary, and that the junior officers in each company had several lengths of rope wound round their bodies, ready to bind prisoners and hostages.

An interesting recollection may be mentioned here. On the morning of 6 January 1781 Betty Le Bourdon was at the house of Rev. George Bertram then rector of St. Clement, where she was a servant. The French invaders used St. Clement's church as a barracks. On the Sunday morning, as she was going to church with Reverend Bertram, she was threatened by a wounded French officer holding an iron bar; she raised her arm to strike him but was stopped by the rector. On their way back from church they saw that the officer had died from his wounds.[1]

De Rullecourt reminded the officers that the war cry was 'Vive le Roi et Luxembourg' and lastly that the platoon commanders were to bayonet without any hesitation any man who made the least noise, thereby betraying their presence. At this last command one of the staff officers showed signs of great satisfaction. He was a very tall man, with a bronze complexion which betrayed his Asiatic origin, and he quivered with pleasure at the prospect of killing so soon to come. This person made an impression on his contemporaries, but his name has been recorded in various forms by historians. He was a gentleman volunteer, who had been promised that he would be a colonel. In the Jersey Museum library is a note in the handwriting of Major Rybot, a Jersey historian, which says 'Emir or Mir Sayad, a common Indian Muslim name'. The French author M. Claretie thought that Emir was a title and not a name and he spoke of the mysterious stranger as Emir Gouas. De Rullecourt, who perhaps did not know the name

THE COLOUR PLATES

Reproduced from paintings by *Henry Fowler*

1(a). (*left*) Private, grenadier company of the 78th Regt., 1781.
1(b). (*right*) Officer, battalion company of the 78th Regt., 1781.

2. Private, 83rd Regt. of Foot,
1781.

3. Sergeant, 95th Regt., 1781.

4. Invalid artilleryman, 17

5. Officer, Jersey Militia infantry,
1781.

7. Gunner, Royal Jersey Militia,
1781.

6. Grenadier, Jersey Militia, 1781.

8. French sergeant of the Regt. of Nassau, 1781.   9. French soldier of the Regt. of Nassau, 1781.

exactly, called his subordinate 'Emire Joad'. However, what is known for sure about this man is that he came from Hindustan, where he had commanded 6,000 horsemen for the Grand Mogul, and that he had held a high rank. In order to learn about the art of war, and spurred on by his hate for the British (whose presence in India he despised), he soon found an opportunity to travel to Europe, and joined the Luxembourg Legion as a volunteer.

The costume which the Turk—as this is what he was usually called—wore, was no more sure than his name. According to contemporary newspapers he retained the Mogul costume, but 'it was made of a blue dolman, uniform colour of the legion, to which he had added epaulettes of his rank, Lieutenant-Colonel; on his turban he had a band of green material, indicating his descent from Mahomet'. The uniform which M. Claretie ascribed to him, according to an English news-paper, is quite different. He was dressed in long trousers of blue material, a shirt of black and white velvet, a tunic in light red, like a dressing gown tied around his belt with a silk cord, which held a scimitar and dagger. On his head was a bonnet with a turban of yellow and white silk, of which the ends fell on his left shoulder. In place of buttons he had rich frogs and loops with silver pendants'. In the interest of the picturesque let us hope that this was the splendid outfit of Emir Said.

De Rullecourt wrote from Chausey to the Chevalier de Luxembourg about his Asiatic officer: 'Emire Joad adapts himself to our wartime life and to the ladies whom he meets on the way. I have promised him a seraglio in Jersey; we have spoken of it so much that he feels he is awaiting hours in the paradise of Mahommet. For his part he says he will drink your health for each English head that he cuts off'.

At La Rocque about a hundred of the most reliable men were left to guard the cannon which had been captured and turned towards the country. They had orders to guard the few remaining boats and to help the retreat should this be necessary. The rest of the columns regrouped near a rock named Perron Côrnet or Cônet, which lay between the parishes of Grouville and St. Clement, and then marched via the Rue du Prince towards St. Helier:[2] 'we have passed in front of five or six forts', de Boislandry wrote later, 'which were truly very ill guarded, as they did not molest us'. On reaching the outskirts of St. Helier the column divided, one taking the high and one the low road.

Meanwhile, in France Régnier was prey to the greatest uncertainty. When his boat got back to Chausey, loaded with the utensils and tools that he had obtained from Granville, the islands were silent and deserted as everyone had left several hours earlier. M. de Graffeton and two other officers, whose names are not known, were with Régnier and they pressed him ardently to take to sea and head for Jersey. This he did, and day was beginning to break when they arrived near the coast; at the moment of landing they were startled by the sound of a canon fired from a fort at St. Clement. Régnier's first thought was that the French had been discovered, but as nothing more happened he thought that it was the normal dawn cannon firing. So he continued, but a little later it started to fire again. This time it was Elizabeth Castle that sounded the alarm and soon all the forts in the district replied to this signal.

Régnier hesitated no more; without stopping to see if he could be of any assistance to the expedition, and presuming that it was of the greatest conse-quence to announce the landing and hasten assistance, he turned to his ship and headed for Granville. Feron's account is different: 'In the morn of 6th Jan. Régnier bringing the order to the *Pilote des Indes* in Jersey approached Elizabeth Castle and met *L'Epreuvier* and *Serin* coming from La Rocque (leaving behind the sloop *Folkestone*). They announced that the embarkation had taken place at 4 a.m. Régnier returned in haste to Granville for help'.

General Dumouriez sent his major from Cherbourg to Carteret to get the news. All the French coast was alerted. M. de Ségur sent couriers to the Duc d'Harcourt on 10 January; he ordered 'that the King's intention was to send to Jersey 1,000 men under the orders of Mons. de la Rozière, in supposing that the Luxembourg volunteers were masters of Elizabeth Castle and St. Aubin's Fort'. It was not until the 15th that news of the defeat reached the French court.

Among the invaders were certain civilians, including Louis Gallien from Bréhat, a merchant who had worked all his life in trade with the islands. However, he was an unknown quantity and the Baron had him watched carefully by Lieutenant Ganne, armed with a pistol in his hand. Finally, the Clerceaux brothers escorted the detachment.

Although there is no proof, it is possible that these were the same men who on Christmas Eve, when de Rullecourt had hoped to surprise the Jersey people in the midst of their festivities, signalled from the coasts of the island and of Normandy to advise the Baron that no British ship was stationed in the district and that he could come without risk. It is known that fires were seen that night by the guards of Trinity and Rozel and at La Coupe, and that replies came from the French coast.[3] On nearing the area of La Dicq the column halted near 'Parker's' house, on hearing cannon fire. John Parker was the publican of what is now the *White Horse* inn.

Chapter X

EVENTS IN ST. HELIER

THE PROGRESS of the French troops became faster as they approached St. Helier, and whilst they were proceeding through Colomberie a young girl called Elizabeth Messervy asked them from an upper storey window,'Ou donc est la garde?' ('Where are the guards?') They replied, 'Elle dorme, ma chérie'. ('They are sleeping, my dear.') They arrived at the first houses in St. Helier at about 6 a.m. From La Rocque to St. Helier they had remained unobserved. Whilst they were passing through the area of Colomberie and Hill Street, Pierre Arrivé came out of his house and was bayoneted to death.[1] French soldiers smashed the doors of the houses of Miss Bazin and Mr. Gosset,[2] also breaking into the public house of Thomas Thacker and the library (then in Library Place), where the librarian, Jacques Limbour, was still in bed. These two men were bound and dragged outside.

Jean de Ste. Croix was inhumanly treated by the French. On hearing the noise in the morning he believed it to be caused by the inhabitants. He took his sword and went to the Market Place, where he was arrested by a French officer who led him to be guarded, telling the soldiers not to treat him gently. In saying these words the officer gave him two blows with his sabre, one cutting his cheek and part of his ear and the other taking the skin off the back of his head. In falling to the ground Jean de Ste. Croix received a bayonet thrust from a soldier: he remained there for a time pretending to be dead, but later, gathering his strength, he dragged himself to a neighbouring house where he had his wounds treated.[3]

Frederick de la Taste, who lived in the Market Place, heard the commotion and came into the street, thinking that it was the 'Glasgow' men of the 83rd Regiment going to market. He was the first witness at the subsequent trial of Major Corbet. Joshua Le Gros, looking out of his window, was struck by a French soldier wielding a halberd. On reaching the Market Place one sentry at the old Picquet House, then opposite Church Street, was put to death. All were disarmed and bound, but another of the sentries escaped and raised the alarm at the hospital barracks, where the 78th Regiment of Highlanders was stationed.[4]

Captain Charleton, the elderly Commander of the Invalids (artillerymen), was captured in the Market Place on coming out of his house wearing a nightcap and slippers. Pierre Amiraux, the noted Jersey silversmith, was also taken near the statue of George II:[5] they were tied together by the wrists and ordered to lead the French to the house of Lieutenant-Governor Corbet, going via what are now King Street (Rue de Derrière), Queen Street (Rue-ès-Porcqs) and La Motte Street, the latter then being open fields.

Corbet was half dressed when Captain Clement Hemery of the Militia artillery arrived to alert him. Hemery had himself been disturbed by the noise, and going to his window saw the French in the street; as his house, now the Chamber of Commerce building, was surrounded, he dressed in his civilian clothes and escaped by going to his cellar and making his exit through a grating into Morier Lane.[6] The Governor's house, at the corner of what is now Grosvenor Street and St. James Street, remained peacefully unaware of events until Captain Hemery arrived at about the same time as Captain Edward Coombes, whose father, seeing Pierre Amiraux and Captain Charleton being tied, had quickly instructed his son to inform the Governor. Naturally Corbet was extremely surprised; he immediately ordered a horse to be saddled, and sent Captain Hemery to ride and warn Captain Campbell of the 83rd Regiment, who was in the barracks at Fort Conway, Grouville.[7] There appears to be no evidence as to who warned Peirson and the 95th at 'La Hougue', St. Peter, who might have heard the alarm guns.

Scarcely had Hemery left when the French surrounded the Governor's house. Perrot states 'that they were met by Mrs. Corbet who told them in English that she could speak no French, that her husband was not there and that he was in the country with his officers and troops . . .'. They did not believe her and a guard escorted her to the Court House in the Market Place while others searched and soon found Corbet. Corbet finished dressing and, seeing the two prisoners Amiraux and Charleton tied, asked the French officer to release them. This was done and they returned home. Corbet was taken to the Court House escorted by guards.

De Rullecourt arrived at the Court House to find it locked. This threw him into a rage and he demanded the keys, threatening to break down the doors. The keys were brought and, accompanied by some of his officers, with Corbet and the other prisoners, de Rullecourt entered the building, having sent Mrs. Corbet home.

The Baron had greeted his prisoner correctly, the latter being speechless and appearing quite morose. Several Jersey notables had been subjected to the same fate as their leader and were ranged round the French officer, under the guard of soldiers commanded by Emir Said, who, scimitar in hand, awaited de Rullecourt's orders.

De Rullecourt then made his wishes known. He simply wanted the island, together with all military installations, to be handed over immediately, and all arms to be placed in the Court House, in return for which the 'Jersey people would enjoy their property, franchise and liberties, the exercise of their religion etc.'. Having called for a pen he pushed the capitulation document towards the Governor, Moise Corbet, for him to sign. When Corbet exclaimed that he found the contents unacceptable, de Rullecourt became menacing. One witness says that he raised his arms and in a firm and imperious tone said 'I insist, I insist, otherwise the town will be given over to pillage'. Near him was Lieutenant Ganne, a large, brutish man, who became furious; and Emir Said with eyes rolling urged him to wait no longer, but to burn the town and put all the inhabitants to the sword.

De Rullecourt put his watch on the table in front of him. 'I will give you half an hour, after which it will be too late', he threatened. In order to impress the Governor, whose embarrassment was obvious and whose will power was wavering, de Rullecourt went on to say 'that all resistance on the part of the British would be useless'. He lied to him, saying that 'the 4,000 men who had come with him were masters of all the principal points in the island and that larger forces would be arriving each night from Cancale and St. Malo, until it would be quite impossible for the Jerseymen to continue the fight'. He then pretended to give orders to one of his officers to advance further on the town, and then to take a letter which he had just written to France; but there is no evidence that such a letter was ever delivered.

Corbet, much perplexed, endeavoured to gain advice about signing from Jean Durell, the King's Procurer, who refused to sign. At last Corbet reluctantly complied. His signature was accompanied—also with the utmost reluctance— by that of Major Alexander Hogge, the Fort Major. The Court officials present obstinately refused to sign in spite of the menacing attitude of Ganne, de Rullecourt's companion, who stated that, given the order, 'in one hour he would leave nothing standing'. Emir Said continued to adopt a threatening attitude and brandished his scimitar to intimidate the prisoners.

De Rullecourt then deployed his troops in the Market Place near the statue of George II, which he ordered was to be respected. Then he read to the assembled crowd a proclamation which he had prepared in advance, urging the inhabitants to return peacefully to their houses and assuring them that their possessions would be safe and that no harm would come to any who submitted peacefully to the new situation. He added that the shops would be opened, each man to go about his own affairs, but that they should avoid assembling in groups so as not to cause defiance to the soldiers. Indeed, it is likely that the latter, frustrated by not being allowed to pillage as they had been promised, would not have been very accommodating; nor would the officers, especially those whose fury and menaces had forced Corbet and Hogge to sign the capitulation. But the General made sure that the strictest discipline continued among his men. He had taken the new title of General when putting on the red ribbon of the Order of St. Louis, which he said the king had authorised him to wear as soon as he was master of the island.

In the report which appears in *La Chronique Almanach* of 1854 a translation is given of Bentley's miscellany *Les Avant Postes de L'Angleterre,* wherein it is stated that the decoration was the 'Sign of the Order of St. Louis'. Such a decoration did exist, and was a royal and military order of France established by King Louis XIV on 5 April 1693, awarded for military valour or distinguished merit; it was re-confirmed by Louis XV. It is unlikely that any decoration for military valour or distinguished merit would be given to anyone before the action. However, de Rullecourt may have been promised this award to accompany his promotion from Lieutenant-Colonel to General, and he purchased the ribbons or sash in expectation. In his *Histoire de la Bataille de Jersey* Jeune says: 'The Baron took a red cord from his pocket with a commission from Louis XVI naming him General of the army and Governor of Jersey'.

One of the French soldiers who had stolen a silver cup in a neighbouring shop was condemned to die at once and to be cut through with the sword. As he was on his knees to receive the sentence pronounced by his General, the Lieutenant-Governor pleaded for him and so saved his life. The man was to be judged by the ordinary legal court of Jersey when ordered was re-established, and was sent to the town prison in the custody of the gaoler, Edouard Hacquoil.

De Rullecourt was delighted; everything was going as he wished, even better than he had dared to hope. He was Governor of Jersey, both through conquest and by commission from the French king, and wishing to act as such, he invited all the notables to dine with him that day in Corbet's house. (He instructed one, Dolly Giblet (Gibaut?) to purchase a goose for their dinner.)[8] Having placed several sentries and posts in various positions, he replaced his sword in its scabbard as a precaution and took a walk in the main street, now called Broad Street. Tradition goes so far as to say that, beguiled by the attractions of a young girl, he bought several ells of ribbon in her shop. At about this time his troops were cutting down banisters in various houses around the Market Place to prevent anyone coming down.[9]

While Corbet was being pressed to sent out the capitulation orders to the island's troops, a French officer entered the court and told de Rullecourt that from the belfry of the town church he could see British troops assembling on Mont Patibulaire (now Westmount). This news made de Rullecourt furious. He turned on Corbet and accused him of deliberately gaining time and said that if he did not dispatch the surrender orders within minutes he would raze the town with fire and sword. The Lieutenant-Governor acceded and dispatched the following order:

> To the Officer commanding the 78th Regiment, St. Helier, 6th January 1791.
>
> The island having been surprised, and to save destruction of the town, and to obtain certain advantages for the inhabitants, the Lieutenant-Governor has signed a capitulation; the troops will leave with all honours of war, the Militia will remain quiet and hostilities will cease.—M. Corbet.

Lieutenant William Nivon of the 83rd Regiment was sent with a French officer to deliver this capitulation note to Gallow's Hill at about 11 a.m.

The messenger, who took another order to the barracks at the general hospital, found a number of officers there. An order to surrender all arms to the Court House was received with violent protests; it exempted bayonets, but said that soldiers were to remain in their quarters, waiting until there were enough boats ready to take the whole garrison back to England. Some thought that the Governor's orders must be obeyed in spite of everything, and others that the capitulation should be ignored and that it was necessary to advance on the enemy at once. The latter won the day.

Chapter XI

EVENTS AT LA ROCQUE

ON HIS WAY BACK from warning the posts and forts as far as Mont Orgueil castle, Captain Clement Hemery of the Royal Jersey Artillery was observed by a party of French soldiers and captured. He was placed under guard in one of the French flat-bottomed boats in shallow water at La Rocque when his captors were themselves assailed by fire of a group of militiamen. Hemery proposed going to parley with the militiamen 'to save unnecessary bloodshed', and upon this ruse being accepted he released himself and returned to St. Helier to report to Corbet; but on seeing Corbet's house surrounded by French troops he made his way to Gallows Hill and joined Peirson's forces. In the letter Hemery wrote to Madame de Carteret in Southampton there is an account of Reverend François Le Couteur, rector of St. Martin's, who was awakened at 7.30 in the morning of 6 January to be informed that alarm guns were firing all over the island. Then John Laugeé, the Jersey nailmaker, arrived breathlessly and told him that the town was full of French troops. Laugeé had narrowly escaped with his life as he had been bayoneted in the breast, and he opened his shirt to show Le Couteur the wound. Le Couteur got ready the guns in his church.[1]

The excuse for keeping weapons of war in the house of God was that 'it was a divine duty to defend one's country'. Le Couteur assisted in taking the guns of St. Martin to La Rocque, and in many accounts (including evidence at the trial of Moise Corbet) the guns were referred to as belonging personally to Le Couteur, who had bought them after the French scare of 1779. Le Couteur continues his narrative: 'We moved toward Fort Conway in Grouville Bay to join a detachment of the East Regiment of Militia and the Glasgow Volunteers. I then being on horseback proceeded to reconnoitre the enemy shipping'. He returned to encourage the 83rd Regiment to attack the French at Platte Rocque and they split into two groups.[2] Most accounts suggest that the attack at La Rocque commenced after Peirson's note for assistance had been received (see page 61).

Le Couteur placed his artillery upon an eminence to bombard the French. The story is now taken up by an extract from the *Glasgow Mercury*. 'Capt. Campbell, commanding officer of the 83rd Regt. having reconnoitred the French post, found that there was a number of men left to guard the battery that they had captured. Campbell brought the Grenadier company which he divided, one half he commanded with a subaltern, the other was commanded by Lieutenant James Robertson, and 10 militiamen under Lieutenant Helier

Godfray. Captain Campbell and his men stationed themselves behind a wall in front of the enemy and sent Lieutenant Robertson to attack their flank. Robertson brought up his 40 men within eight or ten yards and ordered the French to surrender, which they refused; they then fired and killed a man, upon which Robertson ordered his grenadiers to charge. They did so and in the advance killed 20 of the enemy and fell upon the rest with bayonets and took them prisoner, all this before Captain Campbell could run up to support them'. Seven grenadiers were killed and seven were wounded. The Le Couteur narrative continues: 'We then perceived that the ships were out of reach, and the C.O. Campbell, having thought proper to return to Fort Conway, I remained with the Militia to cannonade a boat that was coming in to take off some of the French that had taken refuge among the rocks which I had the pleasure of driving back without effecting her purpose, causing 14 to be taken prisoner'.[3]

Soon afterwards Le Couteur perceived Lieutenant Snow of the St. Helier Artillery coming from the town to Fort Conway carrying the shameful note of capitulation from the Lieutenant-Governor, which ordered all troops to suspend hostilities.[4] Fired with indignation, Le Couteur urged Campbell to ignore the note, saying that 'as Corbet was a prisoner it carried no authority, and he besought them to march against St. Helier, but Campbell hesitated in disobeying the orders of a superior officer'. Le Couteur then turned his pleas to Lieutenant Robertson, who stated that he dare not disobey as he would lose his commission. Thereupon Le Couteur, who was a wealthy man, guaranteed to indemnify Robertson if this happened. The problem was solved by the arrival of Lieutenant Thomas Anley, who came from Major Peirson with a scrap of paper on which was written 'Make haste to come to our assistance. We are going to engage'. To Le Couteur's joy that determined them to march.[5]

Perrot's account of the action at La Rocque states that 'the French had entrenched themselves inside the redoubt of which they occupied the breastwork in four ranks, aiming their captured cannon at their assailants'. In this action the French lost one officer, and 20 other ranks were killed; one officer and many men were wounded. The dead were later buried at a spot near Platte Rocque House.[6] Lieutenant Helier Godfray was wounded.

In the Société Jersiaise *Bulletin* for 1902 there is a copy of a letter written by Militia Colonel William C. Lemprière of the North Regiment to his father in England, dated 13 February 1781: '. . . the Lieutenant of the 83rd who attacked the French at La Rocque, who it is said is to be promoted, deserves censure not praise. He with a small party jumped over a hedge and attacked an enemy twice in number, when he might have fired from behind the hedge or waited for the other division of the company that was coming another way, thereby saving the lives of several brave soldiers'.

An engraving after P. J. Ouless of 1840 shows this engagement. It portrays the moment when the 83rd, together with a detachment of the East Regiment of Militia, arrived with their colours at the scene of the action, whilst near the coast the invasion can be seen. Contemporary evidence suggests that the only regimental colours carried that day were those of the 95th Regiment and those of the St. Lawrence Battalion of Militia. As the 83rd and 78th Regiments were divided between Jersey and Guernsey their colours would have been retained in Scotland at the regimental headquarters.

Chapter XII

DE RULLECOURT'S FIRST FAILURE

WHEN DE RULLECOURT had finished his leisurely stroll around the town he returned to the Court House. All Corbet's emissaries had completed their missions and returned, but no arms had been deposited. The General showed great surprise and anger, and Corbet, to calm the fury which he saw mounting in his enemy, felt forced to appear to co-operate. It had just been reported that the rector of St. Helier, Reverend Jean du Pré, had refused to give up the arms which were thought to be with him. The Governor declared that du Pré had no arms, and so as to avert attention from the incident ordered the man in charge of the gunstore to open it and to bring the keys to de Rullecourt (this was in the town church, where the cannon were kept). De Rullecourt did not wish to concern himself with such details, as more serious preoccupations began to confront him. Elizabeth Castle, the most important point on the island, was not yet in his grasp.

Meanwhile earlier that morning Captain Mulcaster, Chief Officer of the Corps of Engineers, had heard of the arrival of the French while he was still in his house in town. He hurriedly dressed and rode to the Invalids' barracks near Havre des Pas, but they were closed, and he realised that the men received permission to do their shopping every Saturday morning. Mulcaster (who lived in Queen Street) then rode out to Elizabeth Castle and, being of senior rank, took command, sending a messenger to Captain Lumsdaine of the 78th Regiment at Westmount to ask for reinforcements. Some minutes later a company of the St. Lawrence Regiment of Militia marched into the castle. Behind them was the messenger from Corbet, who as a result of the capitulation brought orders both for a ceasefire and also for the castle garrison to surrender and deposit their arms in the Court House, where they would receive all honours of war. Mulcaster paid little attention to this order, and put the capitulation in his pocket without reading it, saying 'that he did not understand French'. For his part Captain Aylward, second in command of the castle, had replied that as Corbet was not free his orders were of no value at all; that under the circumstances the troops owed obedience to the second in command, Major Peirson, and that for the past honour of the fortress which they occupied—and which it was their duty to defend—the garrison was resolved to fight to the last.

De Rullecourt wished to go to the castle to see the situation for himself. He placed himself at the head of a number of his grenadiers, holding the Lieutenant-

Governor by the arm. The group advanced too slowly for the wishes of Corbet, who several times urged the men forward saying, 'Tell your men to hurry as the approaching tide will bar our passing'. 'We have the time', said de Rullecourt, but immediately gave orders for those at the head of the column to quicken their steps.

On reaching the beach the column was observed by Mulcaster and a castle cannon opened fire. It was out of range, but the second shot wounded two men, one of whom was a lieutenant of the Grenadiers whose leg was severed from his body,[1] and this sight caused complete chaos in the ranks. De Rullecourt was furious. He insulted Corbet and then, shaking with rage, ordered Corbet to write a letter addressed to the officer commanding Elizabeth Castle stating, 'I enclose the capitulation that I have signed to save the town from pillage. The French officer, le Chevalier des Varannes, Captain of the Luxembourg Volunteers, who accompanies Mons. d'Auvergne, is to be given safe conduct and allowed to return immediately'. The first messenger chosen was Charles d'Auvergne, father of the Prince of Bouillon and inspector of military works in the island, who when asked if he could ride answered 'No', so de Rullecourt ordered the Chevalier des Varannes to mount behind d'Auvergne and ride to the castle.

D'Auvergne and the French officer were taken to Captain Mulcaster, who put the two papers in his pocket without reading them, saying again that he did not speak French. He then had the French officer blindfolded and taken to be shown a battery of cannon charged with grapeshot, directed towards the beach, having a deadly effect when discharged at troops advancing in close formation.

The French officer vainly tried to persuade Mulcaster to surrender, and when told of the 10,000 French troops on their way Captain Mulcaster coldly replied 'All the better, there will be more to kill', and added that he would not surrender the castle 'as long as there was one man left standing'. When de Rullecourt received this account, on the return of the French officer, he again had a fit of rage. So far all had gone well for him and this was his first real setback. With the rising of the tide de Rullecourt and his party returned to St. Helier, observing the increasing number of troops massing on the heights of Mont Patibulaire and realising that he must fortify his position at all costs, for his artillery had not yet arrived. Indeed it was never to arrive, for once again the sea had aided the islanders. De Rullecourt sent one of his officers, M. de Stetenhoff, to La Rocque to hurry their artillery and troops to the town, as he knew he would need all available men, but because of the falling tide Major d'Herville had been unable to disembark his artillery and he returned to France with the majority of his force.

Facing determined hostility, the Baron did not push forward. He returned to the Market Place, although more and more soldiers could be seen assembling on Mont Patibulaire. These were men of Captain Lumsdaine's regiment, who had rushed there as soon as they heard the first news of a French attack, together with Militia battalions of St. Lawrence, St. Saviour, St. Ouen, and St. Mary, the South West and North Militia Regiments and the 95th Regiment. They had brought all the cannon they possessed and such was the haste that Peirson himself helped to harness the horses.

Whilst the regulars and militia were assembling on Mont Patibulaire a startling incident occurred. As the men were falling in a youth on horseback was seen approaching at full speed, and drawing up in front of the St. Lawrence battalion he was recognised as the son of Francis Le Sueur. He had brought his father's pistols, thinking that he had forgotten them.[2]

As soon as he returned to the Market Place de Rullecourt gave instructions to place the militia cannon he had taken from the arsenal in the town church to cover the exits of the Market Place; but even though he called for volunteers he did not have enough experienced soldiers to man them, as none of his artillerymen or guns had been able to land at the time of disembarkation. He later arranged his men in battle order, and placed barricades across Hill Street. In spite of everything, de Rullecourt was still optimistic. After his early triumph he did not wish to admit to the sad reversal of his fortunes which events now foretold. He hoped that the letter which Corbet had just written to the forces grouped on the high land at Mont Patibulaire would persuade them to retire. The Lieutenant-Governor had sent this letter without deceiving himself as to its results, but, as he stated later, with the secret hope of gaining time.

Chapter XIII

THE ATTACK ON THE MARKET PLACE

ON MONT PATIBULAIRE deliberations continued. In a council of war, the senior officers of the British regulars and the Jersey Militia decided unanimously to delay no longer, to attack the French (who were cut off in the Market Place) and to purge the whole island of its invaders. None of them doubted that this would involve serious risks, and everyone foresaw a difficult march through the narrow streets, which could be raked by the fire of the enemy, whose strength and numbers were unknown. Alarm of the invasion had been given to the inhabitants by the firing of cannon and ringing of church bells, each Militiaman rushing to a pre-arranged rendezvous.

The men of the St. Lawrence battalion under Colonel George Benest were impatient and wanted to attack the town while de Rullecourt was parleying near Elizabeth Castle, and his forces were divided, but Captain Lumsdaine held them back. By 10.30 a.m. the greater part of the Militia was assembled. The St. Martin's division had gone to attack the enemy at Grouville and Captain Lumsdaine sent Charles Lemprière to ride and order them to join him at Mont Patibulaire. Several Jerseymen, among them Captain William (?) Patriarche and Hamon, escaped from their French guards in the Market Place, joined up with the British forces, and were given arms.

Major Francis Peirson, barely 24 years old, and the son of Francis Peirson of Mawthorpe, Yorkshire, had only become a major the previous April, when he came to Jersey with the 95th Regiment of Infantry. The French author M. Claretie says that 'he was a handsome young man, beardless, a high forehead, a fine mouth, a gentle air, with great charm'. This is confirmed in the miniature by Philippe Jean, the Jersey painter: 'a high white cravat, fair hair knotted behind, a calm smile on his honest and sensitive lips, an open look, profound, penetrating and thoughtful'.

The thought of finding such a chance to distinguish himself so early in his career filled Peirson with enthusiasm, and he at once took all the necessary steps to ensure success. As a result of an inexplicable oversight de Rullecourt had not occupied the hill which dominated the town. Peirson sent a party of the North Militia Regiment there, with some companies of the 78th and 95th, commanded by a Highlander, Captain Fraser, and guided by one Thomas Pipon, the military storekeeper, with orders to descend on the town when he himself began the attack. Then, putting himself at the head of his troops, he gave the signal for departure.

The British column descending Mont Patibulaire was met by a French officer bearing a white handkerchief on the top of his sword. Peirson halted his force and was told by the officer that he had come from Corbet and de Rullecourt with the capitulation document which ordered Peirson to surrender his forces and deposit their arms in the Royal Court. To this Peirson indignantly replied in French: 'Yes, we will carry our arms to the Court House but there will be a bayonet on the end of every musket'. The French officer asked to be allowed one hour to return and convey Peirson's remarks to his leader. The Militia officers urged Peirson to attack immediately before the enemy could organise a defence; but Peirson resisted their entreaties and, wanting to be sure that Corbet was really a prisoner, ordered two officers, Ensign Charles Byne and Adjutant Harrison of the 95th Regiment, to accompany the French officer back to de Rullecourt and tell him 'that neither the Militia or the regular troops that he commanded will surrender under any conditions and that if the Lieutenant-Governor was indeed a prisoner he was to be released immediately'.

He gave them half an hour to accomplish their mission. On arriving at the Court House the three officers found Corbet and de Rullecourt with several local inhabitants. The British officers asked de Rullecourt 'if Corbet was a prisoner?' 'No', he replied in bad English, 'you can see he still carries his sword.' Corbet then explained that he had been surprised in bed and had been obliged to sign the capitulation to save the island and its inhabitants and ensure the safety of his army. He then read to Adjutant Harrison the following note: 'Major Peirson, you are ordered with the troops under your command to go to the Hospital Barracks; there you will pile your arms and return to "La Hougue" and remain there until a fleet arrives from England. You can keep your colours and the officers their swords'. Meanwhile, Peirson, disturbed at the time that his two emissaries were taking, sent another officer to hasten their return.

Corbet, always under the impression that the burning of the town was imminent, made a last effort to avert disaster by asking de Rullecourt to allow him to go in person to appeal to Peirson. De Rullecourt, playing his last card, allowed him to go, accompanied by a French officer under a flag of truce, and the party of English and French officers moved off to contact Peirson, who had not yet continued his advance. Two eye-witnesses have reported on the meeting, Corbet saying to Peirson: 'Sir, I was taken by surprise this morning'. 'Sir', replied Peirson, 'I want you to know that the 78th and the 95th have not been surprised as yet.'

Corbet then told Ensign Byne to read the articles of capitulation. When this was finished Peirson said to Corbet: 'Then you are a prisoner'. 'Yes', replied Corbet.

'The officers and men have decided to defend the island and show their loyalty to their King and country.'

'Major Peirson, resistance is useless, there are now in St. Helier, 1,000 men, 2 battalions of artillery with their guns, 6,000 men or more have landed on the other side of the island and 10,000 men await orders at St. Malo.'

Peirson asked the Lieutenant-Governor for proof of this statement, and Corbet, placing his hand on his heart said: 'I confirm this on my honour', but on an instant's reflection further stated, 'Sir, I have as a guarantee the word of the French General'.

Peirson concluded: 'We have decided to defend the island for as long as we live; how long do you need to return to St. Helier?'.

'Twenty minutes', replied Corbet. At this, several officers of the Militia and regulars cried, 'Ten minutes is sufficient', and Peirson, holding his watch, said, 'Sir, return to the town and advise the French General that in ten minutes I will attack'. The Lieutenant-Governor and the French officers had hardly left when Peirson drew his sword. At once the bearskin caps of the Grenadiers and the Militiamen's hats were raised as a sign of enthusiasm, and three vigorous hurrahs greeted the order to march. The young commander placed himself in front of his men, his watch in his hand, and after ten minutes he advanced with his men into the town, through Les Mielles, past the hospital and under the archway of the prison which was then at Charing Cross.

The column advanced with Peirson leading. On reaching the division between Broad Street and King Street Peirson divided his force into two columns. One, under the command of Captain Lumsdaine with the 78th Regiment, the Militia battalions from St. Lawrence, St. Ouen and some companies from St. John, approached what is now Vine Street. On arrival they were fired upon by the cannon which de Rullecourt had positioned at the bottom of the Market Place facing Broad Street. Fortunately, due to the inexperience of the French amateur gunners, the shot flew harmlessly over their heads.[1] Colonel Thomas Pipon of the South West Militia[2] and his men also marched up La Grande Rue (Broad Street) towards the Market Place.

The other column led by Peirson marched up King Street with the 95th Regiment, followed by the rest of the Militia. At the side of Peirson, who advanced on foot, rode Charles Lemprière, who had been charged with carrying orders to the troops behind. Peirson reached the small street, Avenue du Marché (now known as Peirson Place) which then contained only two houses, one on the left[3] which was owned by Dr. Philippe Lerrier, and one on the right[4] owned by the Patriarche family. Also at Peirson's side was Adjutant Harrison, who implored him to change his exposed position as he was certain to be hit, but Peirson just smiled, crossed the street and pointed with his sword to the new position which a group of his Grenadiers were to take. At this moment, a French soldier posted near the angle of a wall fired and shot the gallant major in the chest. He died in the arms of his Grenadiers without saying a word, and was carried into the house of Mrs. Fiott. Perrot records that Peirson's death was avenged by a Jersey Militiaman and Peirson's black servant, who was called 'Pompey'.

Following the death of their Commander the British troops were momentarily confused. They were forced back to an area[5] which was the courtyard of the house of Thomas Durell the Vicomte, Colonel of the St. Helier Regiment. The soldiers were rallied and encouraged by young Lieutenant Philippe Dumaresq[6] of the St. Peter's battalion of Militia, assisted by a sergeant of the 95th Regiment. Taking courage, these troops soon regained lost ground and once more reached the entrance of the Market Place. Meanwhile Captain Fraser, who had occupied the Town Hill, saw the action in the Market Place and did not hesitate. Leaving the Militia to command the heights he descended with the regular troops into Hill Street and thence by two small streets into the Market Place. Having advanced up Broad Street Captain Lumsdaine entered the Market Place, so as to cover the French from all corners!

The battle raged fiercely and the noise from the musket fire was deafening. Bullets were whizzing everywhere, for not only were the combatants in the Market Place firing but their fire was also joined by the Militia firing down from the Town Hill. Mrs. Fiott, the wife of Nicholas, who lived in one of the houses[7] overlooking the Market Place, received a musket ball in the arm whilst looking out of her window,[8] slightly wounding her. It was to her house that the body of Peirson was carried.

Soon the numerical superiority of the British made itself felt, although the French fought bravely. De Rullecourt came out of the Court House holding the arm of Lieutenant-Governor Corbet and, according to one account, holding three swords by their points as a token of surrender. On seeing this a group of soldiers of the 78th Regiment opened fire, two balls going through the Governor's hat and four striking the French General. One shattered his jaw, one went through his neck and two penetrated his thigh. De Rullecourt was carried into Dr. Philippe Lerrier's house[9] and died six hours later without having uttered a word.

Seeing that resistance was impossible, the French officers entreated Corbet to reassume command of the British troops and order them to cease firing. This was accomplished only with difficulty, as the British troops and Militia, possibly elated with victory, did not immediately obey the cease fire order, even though the flag of victory had been raised on the Court House. One whose behaviour is recorded was Emir Said. 'Seeing all was lost and that he would in all probability be slain, he threw himself to the ground in front of the Court House steps, acted as if he was wounded and howled in agony, and thus saved himself from the vengeance of those he had terrorised throughout the morning'.

The battle lasted for nearly a quarter of an hour, and it was now half past twelve. Lieutenant-Governor Corbet, having re-established his authority, ordered the rounding up of over four hundred prisoners and placed them in the town church under guard of members of the St. Lawrence battalion of Militia. Officers were imprisoned in the Royal Court House.

Unsure of events at La Rocque, Corbet ordered the Militia to proceed there at once. However, those of the enemy that Lieutenant Robertson and his men had not killed or taken prisoner had joined their comrades, who had been prevented from landing by contrary winds and tide, and had returned in their boats to the safety of France. Many others hid in the Jersey countryside for several days. Because of the danger of further attack if de Rullecourt's threat was true, the Militia and regulars were obliged to keep a sharp lookout all night. A commotion was caused by gunfire in the middle of the night at sea. The prisoners in the town church yelled at the top of their voices for deliverance, but it was a false alarm caused by a cutter coming from Guernsey who fired to give warning of its arrival.

Although the action had been short and comparatively small numbers of troops were engaged, the losses were severe. Seventy-eight French were killed and 80 wounded, eight of whom died during the first night in hospital. Of the British regulars 12 died and 36 were wounded; of the Militia four died and 29 were wounded. Many different accounts of losses exist. Tradition says that the majority of French dead, including the six wounded who died in the general hospital, were buried in a common grave behind the hospital (now Kensington Place). Among the first convoy of prisoners to leave for England were: Le Chevalier d'Herbouville, Le Chevalier Ferrant, Le Sieur St. George de Bonnechose, Lieutenant Porlier and Capitaine de Bétancourt. These officers were wounded and in the charge of Piatte, the assistant surgeon. After various French troops had surrendered or been rounded up from all over the island, it is stated that a total of 456 officers, N.C.O.s and men were made prisoner.

Had the initial attack by de Rullecourt been successful, a further invasion force of 3,200 men would have been massed and ready to embark at Granville and St. Malo, comprising 1,000 men of the Régiments de Berwick and d'Auvergne; 1,800 men of the Régiments Royale Roussillon, Royal Corse and d'Aquitaine; 200 men with artillery and munitions of the Legion de Nassau plus the 285 men with artillery, howitzers and munitions who were the original rear guard at La Rocque. All these were under the orders of Monsieur de la Rozière, commandant of St. Malo. And so it should be appreciated that, short and restricted as the initial attack was, had it not been for the determined resistance of men like Peirson and Mulcaster, the outcome would have been very different. Had de Rullecourt been successful there was clearly no shortage of reinforcements ready to arrive from France. England might then have found it hard to evict an entrenched enemy without doing great harm to the inhabitants' lives and property, as was the case in the Second World War.

Chapter XIV

THE AFTERMATH IN JERSEY

Major Francis Peirson's Funeral, 10 January 1781, at 2 p.m.

The cortège was as follows:

95th Regiment officers. Colours, halberds, all in mourning with arms reversed.

Three captains, 6 lieutenants, all the ensigns off duty, 12 sergeants, 12 corporals, 10 drummers, all the fifers, and 300 men.

Drum major, sashed and scarfed.

Officers of the artillery, scarfed.

Two pieces of cannon.

Regimental surgeon-general.

Regimental surgeon's mate.

The Major's horse, clothed and decorated in deep mourning, boots and spurs reversed, led by two servants in long cloaks.

The clergy of the Island.

The chaplain, the dean and the regimental chaplain, in scarfs.

The coffin, supported by the oldest officers of the garrison.

Captain James Corbet (chief mourner as next in command to Peirson).

Lieutenant-Governor and Lieutenant Bailiff.

The Jurats.

Officers of the Royal Court.

The gentlemen of the Island.

The officers of the Invalids.

The body, in a lead coffin, was deposited under the Governor's pew in a brick vault in St. Helier's parish church in front of the pulpit. A copper plate was placed on the coffin, which read: 'The remains of Major Francis Peirson who by his courage and conduct rescued the island of Jersey from the hands of a rapacious enemy the sixth day of January 1781, are here deposited. He fell at the head of his conquering troops in the 25th year of his age'.

The model figure of Major Peirson now in the Jersey Museum was made by Jerseyman William Henry Sohier, and was first placed on view in the States Committee[1] room in September 1873. In August 1819 the first member of Peirson's family to visit Jersey after the battle was Arthur Anstey, who married one of Peirson's sisters;[2] He left the island on 28 August 1819.

Major Peirson had a black servant or batman (which was not unusual at this period), whose name was Pompey. It is recorded that at the time of Major Peirson's death Pompey avenged his master and shot the French assailant. In the papers of the Fiott family published by the Société we read that one day Pompey turned up in London at the premises of Mr. Fiott and asked for work, explaining his connection with the Battle of Jersey. Mr. Fiott engaged him, but unfortunately had to dismiss him later 'as an incorrigible drunkard'. We last hear of Pompey going to York to find Peirson's family.

Under the heading of 'Yorkshire in the last Century—Old History retold', the *Yorkshire Gazette* published a diary containing events of interest. The following appeared on 1 June 1790: 'The black servant of the late Major Peirson applied at the Mansion House, York, for relief, having travelled with a pass from Portsmouth to visit the parents of his excellent master. The poor man went from Jersey to Portsmouth, where he was pressed, but on making his case known to the captain of the *Barfleur* he was instantly set at liberty and a pass to York was provided for him. On arriving in the city he found that the parents of his late master had been dead for some time, which greatly affected him, and he was thrown upon the generosity and compassion of the public. His portrait was introduced in a picture painted by Copley, to commemorate the gallantry of Major Peirson in one of the most trying situations that ever fell to the lot of a young man officer. Contributions to assist the distressed man were received at the York banks to enable him to provide clothing and the means of returning to Jersey'.

The dying de Rullecourt was carried into the house of Doctor Philippe Lerrier, where it is said that the stain of blood flowing from his wounds remained for many years on the flagstones. In spite of the great care taken of him (this was recognised by his widow, who gave Lerrier a gold box decorated with a miniature and previous stones), Baron de Rullecourt died during the evening and was buried the following day with the full military honours due to his rank. The bearers were his own officers and he was laid to rest outside the old west door of the parish church of St. Helier, less than one hundred yards from where he fell. At the head of his grave a small stone bearing his name was replaced in 1871 by a square block of granite bearing the simple words 'de Rullecour 6th of January 1871'. His coffin was supplied by Amice Norman, an architect and master carpenter, for £12, and Pierre Mallet lined it in black plush at a cost of eight pounds.

In March 1781 a letter from John Fiott in London to his father Nicholas in Jersey says 'de Rullecourt's children are to be admitted into the French Protestant Refugees School in London'.[3]

Armed detachments were ordered to round up the French troops who were in hiding or endeavouring to reach La Rocque, for they were unaware that there were no ships to take them back to the safety of France. French officers who received serious wounds in the course of the day were the Captains de Betancourt, Captain Commandant of the Bombadiers of Luxembourg (his wounds being fatal), the Chevalier Ferrant (who had a crushed foot), the Chevalier d'Herbouville and Lieutenants St. George de Bonnechose and Porlier, who were taken to hospital.

Several persons who were named in papers seized from de Rullecourt and suspected of having connived with him were arrested. Firstly there was Pierre Journeaux who was put in prison, and secondly Edouard Millais, who had escaped but was captured the next night, and who was incarcerated in Elizabeth Castle and then taken to England until May 1871, when he was released for lack of evidence.

Captain Leroux,[4] a Frenchman, was also imprisoned, although the only charge against him was that he married a woman from St. Lawrence Valley, which suggested that he might have had dealings with the French. It is fair to add that in imprisoning Leroux the authorities were not entirely to blame, although they had no certain proof that this man, who had remained with the English after a case of fraud against *les Fermiers-Genéraux,* was a dangerous enemy to them. As a pilot Leroux commanded a group of privateers from Jersey cruising in the Channel, protected by the vessel *Jupiter*; he was one of the spies employed by Régnier, who promised to obtain letters of pardon for him in exchange for his services. He had to report to him all he knew about squadrons or convoys ready to leave, and their destination; and more than once Régnier, disguised as a fisherman, went to confer with Captain Leroux on board a 14-gun corsair which the latter commanded.

At St. Helier the dead and wounded of both sides were being moved. A grave in a corner of Grouville churchyard held the British victims of the combat at La Rocque, but their enemies lie without a stone to indicate their resting place.[5]

Nassau's abortive attempt against Jersey had, as mentioned, aroused the government, and General Conway, Governor of the Island, had been concerned to take precautions to prevent any new risk in the future. Owing to him the Militia had been called upon to drill more frequently, and work on fortifications was speeded up. When he thought that all was in good order the General returned to England. He had installed himself a few months previously in his property at Park Place, Henley. Early in the morning of 9 January he received a message from the Council which stupified him. Lieutenant Richard Adderton of the 95th Regiment, who had been sent by Major Peirson, arrived from Jersey during the night, bringing the news that the French had landed. The messenger had come at great speed to ask for prompt help. Ministers urged the General to return to his post in Jersey. He sailed from Portsmouth with troops and transport, but a violent storm caused the loss of a transport and 60 men. After battling two days in the Channel they put into Plymouth, where he heard of the French defeat. Conway became severely ill due to exposure.

The absence of reliable news left the way wide open for rumours which ran their course. The *Morning Chronicle* said that an engineer who had just come from the island was most pessimistic, and that according to him neither the garrison nor Elizabeth Castle could hold out for more than 10 hours. The paper commented upon news brought by messengers from Jersey and communications from the Admiralty, saying that doubtless the official sources hid part of the truth so as not to alarm the populace. New messengers arrived all the time, including a vessel sent in haste from Mont Orgueil Castle, to warn Sir Thomas Pye, Governor of Portsmouth, of the French arrival in Jersey. In 1782 the States paid Thomas Filleul 13 guineas for this service, three for himself and two each for the five men who accompanied him. Pye sent this information to London at once by two his his lieutenants.

Public opinion demanded energetic measures to be taken. The Council sent Captain James Wallace to collect and send forth important reinforcements—two regiments of infantry, the 14th and 97th, with a large detachment of marines, in the vessels, *Nonesuch, Buffalo* and *Romney,* three frigates, two sloops and four cutters. A letter sent from Southampton on 9 January states that when the Dorsetshire Militia heard of the French attack they asked their colonel to use his influence to permit them to leave immediately for St. Helier. He reluctantly refused, reminding them of the Act of Parliament which did not permit militiamen to leave the kingdom.

Corbet's court martial began at the Horse Guards in London on 1 May. He was not charged with treason as some writers have stated, but 'that he did contrary to his duty and the trust reposed in him, sign with the Commander of the French Troops articles of capitulation, although the enemy had become masters only of the town of St. Helier, and Elizabeth Castle as well as the other forts were still in custody of His Majesty's troops; and further, that he did endeavour to induce others shamefully to abandon and deliver to the French the several forts and posts committed to their charge'. Major Corbet was tried by three generals, four colonels and eight lieutenant-colonels. The trial lasted five days, the verdict being: 'The Court are of the opinion that Moise Corbet be superceeded in his commission as Lieutenant-Governor'. He was granted a pension of £250 per annum, which was the full pay of a serving major in the British army. Corbet was relieved of his command and replaced by Colonel John Reid of the 95th Regiment, who was sworn in as Lieutenant-Colonel on 17 January 1781. Corbet lived in seclusion, and some say that he died in France in 1817, at the age of eighty-nine. At the trial the absence from the island of the three commanding officers and their subordinates from the three garrison regiments, who were on Christmas leave, was not mentioned.

A subscription was opened in Jersey after the battle to assist the victims, and 8,000 livres were collected. Each widow received three Louis d'or;[6] two

Louis d'or were given to each child of a man killed or seriously wounded; five were given to each man grievously wounded, and three to each man slightly wounded. Double these sums was paid to soldiers of the Militia.

The commander of La Rocque Tower, Sergeant Falle, was taken to court on 17 January with eight of his men and charged with neglect of duty. He was imprisoned and his men were cautioned. Edouard Godfray, a Militiaman of the St. Lawrence battalion, was taken to court for being absent from his post on 6 January and was sentenced to 15 days' imprisonment on bread and water; irons were to be attached to his legs. An Act of Court ordained the latter sentence to be 'read out in front of the regiments'. It is said that Major Alexander Hogge, Commander of the Island's forts, who with Corbet had signed the capitulation, died of a broken heart. He was buried near de Rullecourt in St. Helier's parish churchyard on 28 November 1782.

Less than two months after they were brought to England a certain number of French officers were returned to France. Among them were Le Chevalier d'Aubrey, Grenadier Capitaine; Grenadier Capitaine de Montardat; Le Chevalier de Baudraye, Capitaine Aide-Majeur; M. de Bleyal, Capitaine Aide-Majeur; Pierre Ganne, Lieutenant de Frègate and Commander of the lugger *Le Renard,* and de Saint-Ange, Lieutenant. In April 1782, 252 Legionnaires were returned to Cherbourg after spending 14 months on the convict ships at Portsmouth. Among them was a certain number of militiamen from Haute-Normandie. Le Chevalier Ferrant, a friend of de Rullecourt, was wounded and was cared for by the Lerrier family.

On 22 February the States assembled in the court room at St. Helier, and as proof of their gratitude sent letters to the regiments and the Island Militia; they also sent an official letter of condolence to Major Peirson's father. At their meeting on 22 April they instructed the king's officers, the rector of St. Martin, and the constable of St. Peter's, who were about to leave for England, to make enquiries and to take the necessary steps to have a monument erected to Major Peirson commemorating his bravery, the cost of which was not to exceed £300 sterling.[7] These gentlemen interviewed several artists and finally gave the order to a sculptor, the elder John Bacon, having arranged with him a price of £317 17s. 6d. This monument is in St. Helier's church, where it was ceremonially unveiled in 1784.

Although the people of Jersey honoured with good cause the memory of this young officer, who fell so bravely leading his men, they judged the behaviour of the Lieutenant-Governor Corbet severely. Long after the attack on 6 January, when the events could be regarded dispassionately, it was said to be dangerous to claim that he was anything but a traitor in front of some people. We who can view the situation in perspective may confine ourselves to relating the facts without comment. We have already seen that after the death of de Rullecourt Major Corbet resumed command, but his authority, which had become only nominal, did not last. Those under him regarded him with suspicion and spied on his every movement, so much did they suspect that he was conniving with the enemy for a further offensive. They had him kept in sight until they had further information about his conduct; at last an order came from London on 25 January to put him under arrest.

While the British distributed praise or blame among those who had been involved in de Rullecourt's adventure, France did not appear to have given up hope of conquering the Channel Islands. There was in fact a rumour, in March 1782, that a considerable force of men and ships was being prepared at St. Malo: it was said that it was being assembled in the Bay of the Basques and that it would start for Jersey in the spring. But neither the Prince of Luxembourg nor Captain Régnier, both of whom had taken part in the campaign which had such an inglorious end, were to take part in this expedition.

Chapter XV

THE AFTERMATH IN FRANCE

*The information in this chapter is translated from the works of the French
authors, Brachet, Feron, Claretie and Perrot*

IF DEEP EMOTION was felt in London on learning that the enemy troops had
landed on English territory, concern was no less felt in France, where the news
of the attempt made by the Baron de Rullecourt gradually spread; it was said to
be 'just a simple affair conducted by private individuals, in which the Government
was not concerned'. Nonetheless, it was realised that as soon as the adventure
started, a brisk correspondence took place between the civil and military adminis-
trators in Brittany and Normandy, and that they wrote daily about it to the
military and naval authorities. Thus it is not surprising that once the Legion of
Luxembourg had embarked everyone, for all sorts of reasons, was interested in
its fate. One might be surprised at 'the strength of a handful of men who wished
to conquer the Island of Jersey' without being sure that the weather was on their
side. Certainly people could declare after the defeat that 'only a few friends and
supporters of the Chevalier of Luxembourg and the Baron de Rullecourt could
persuade themselves that the latter would become master of Jersey'.

Nevertheless, there were some who admired this bold action, and even if they
did not expect a happy outcome of the drama they could not help but applaud
the part played by the actor. Commissaire General Guillot wrote: 'Without as yet
knowing what he had done and what had become of him I admire him, still
believing his constancy, perseverance, firmness and how, with a handful of
undisciplined troops, he managed to keep them for eleven days and eleven
nights in open boats and finally to direct them to Jersey'.

While de Rullecourt was landing on the island alarm guns reverberated without
interruption over the sea, reaching the French coast, and leading people to believe
that an important engagement was taking place. This cannonade lasted throughout
the Saturday, doubtless as the victors celebrated their triumph after the battle.
Meanwhile, in the rough seas of that January day the vessels cruising in the area,
the *Pilote des Indes,* the *Folkestone,* and the *Serin,* dared not get near enough
to Jersey to discover the news. On each one of them the lookout man scanned
the horizon in vain, searching for the boats which they thought the Baron could
not fail to send; but nothing appeared. At about 10 o'clock in the evening Captain
Le Tourneur met Régnier's boats and hailed M. Boinard, who was on board. The

latter said that he had come from Jersey, that de Rullecourt had landed with all
his troops and that he had taken the town. On Sunday, at daybreak, all had
changed. Pierre Bouret dit la Rivière, captain of *La Prudente,* who seemed to be
informed, told the commander of the *Pilote des Indes* that the army was beaten,
that some of them had re-embarked, but that the leader and about six hundred
men, being unable to do anything else, had remained prisoners on the rocks.

To quote Le Tourneur: 'I at once sent my boat to inform Mons. Eustache,
Commissaire at Granville and Ryan, the Commandant of the Berwick Regiment,
to warn them that they must make preparations for the assistance that could
be sent and that I was going to get to Cancale to instruct M. Guillot. About two
hours later, a shallop from the *Oiseau* came alongside me; I hauled it on board.
How great was my distress when I saw de Rullecourt's major, who said that I
had been misinformed, that Mons. de Rullecourt was in Jersey, where he was
making war and had great need of help, and that the account which I had heard
could only have come from some of his soldiers from the boat with which I
had spoken and who did not know what was happening, and that it was true that
Mons. de Rullecourt had no more than 700 men, as the Major had not been able
to land with him, and that having suffered hinderances he was going to land at
11 o'clock in the morning, but the enemy had opposed his landing and that two
ketches advanced on him, making him feel it best to re-embark, and that he was
ready to return when he had spoken to the Commissaire at Granville. I urged him
to use all his efforts to arrive in time to stop orders which Mons. Ryan and
Eustache might give after the unfortunate information I had given them. He
left at once. At about 4 in the afternoon I made preparations and left to anchor
at the end of La Rocque de Granville, and following the wishes of the Major of
the Luxembourg Regiment, I ordered all boats not to enter the Port. The said
La Rivière, and another man who was leaving with him, made me fire a shot
of cannon for them . . . at six in the evening as we were anchored at the end
of la Rocque among nine boats of the expedition'.

Little happened as a result of Le Tourneur's involuntary mistake, as the
couriers of Eustache and Colonel de Berwick had not even left Granville. But in
order to cover himself Le Tourneur persuaded all the officers who were present
to sign a declaration of what had happened, and Bachaumont, often harsh and
unjust in the judgements he has left, said that the Major was so terrified that his
hand trembled as he signed.

We know nothing for sure about Régnier's mission. He returned from Jersey
without having even tried to land, and said he had been blown by the winds to the
port of Régneville, and came at once to Granville from there. The news that he
brought, and that couriers took to the commandants of the province, was that
French troops must have occupied St. Helier as he had seen Elizabeth Castle
firing on them, and that a pall of smoke was rising above the town. Lieutenant
Vallée of the *Pilote des Indes* went to find out on Regniér's boat and searched
in vain for a way of landing on the island, but he was chased by an English cutter

and was forced to retire without finding out anything at all. Another attempt made the same day was no more successful. Vallée had to put into Chausey, and was not able to leave again until the next day as the wind was so strong. However, there was no lack of opinions and each man gave his own according to the situation at the moment. Twenty different versions were current, varying from hour to hour, but some people were already beginning to think that there had been a defeat and that de Rullecourt was lost.

One must suppose that this was also the opinion of Major d'Herville, as one cannot find a trace of evidence that he insisted on rejoining his leader as he should have done; he went back to M. Eustache, and as the Commissaire des Classes did not wish to keep the 285 men returning from Chausey at Granville, it was decided to take them to Chausey, where they would await orders from Paris. All the men remained on board the transports, and so one might have hoped that their departure would be accomplished without difficulty, but their lack of discipline had been forgotten.

At about 5 o'clock in the morning on the 8th *l'Oiseau* lifted anchor with d'Herville and Régnier aboard and signalled to the other boats to follow. Most obeyed at once, but some of them remained stationary. The *Corvette* from Granville was called in to hurry them. On the advice of the owner of the *Adelaide* that 40 soldiers whom he had were ready to revolt and refused to set sail, Le Tourneur told them that if they did not at once obey the orders of their officers he would fire on them. So they decided to go. This incident was hardly over when another appeared. M. Dèlpeche, Lieutenant in the Legion of Luxembourg, had embarked at Dieppe on the *St. Laurent*, commanded by François Olivier. As this boat had already sustained some damage they both agreed that she could not make the journey to Chausey, and that they would not leave. Le Tourneur replied that certainly he had no orders to give to the officers, but that he would obey the Major and set sail; as to the owner of the boat, if he refused to take her he would open fire on it. As a result of this firm attitude all resistance was broken and two hours later everyone had left. Régnier returned the same day to Granville, and returned to Chausey the following day in the *Pilote des Indes*; he carried provisions for the Legion and brought back 27 soldiers from the troop that a Régneville boat had left in port. This transit was not without difficulty, as the storm prevented Le Tourneur from landing at Chausey. The soldiers were put into a shallop, which as a result of the strength of the wind was blown on to the rocks and lost, but none of the soldiers was injured. Le Tourneur returned to Granville with some sick men who had been put in his charge by Major d'Herville because they were lacking medical care.

Time passed. By 10 January there was still no news about de Rullecourt; whilst admitting the possibility that after an unexpected landing he had seized St. Helier 'which had no surrounding walls', the Governor of Normandy found it strange that no single eye-witness and not one letter had arrived to confirm the account that Régnier had given to M. Ryan. He said 'that it seems most unlikely that these 600 or 700 men could have caused such terror to the officers and men who comprise the Jersey garrison and its castles, for with the artillery they have to defend themselves, the sea which separates them from the land at high tide, the provisions which have been stored there since the war—that our forces could get there without being attacked, or without even having the appearance of being attacked'.

On the 11th silence and uncertainty continued. All the same, the Sub-Delegate of Coutances repeated a current rumour. A boat which had arrived that day at Carteret reported that the Baron was in a difficult position and that he had lost many men. But this was only a rumour, and boats continued to be sent to reconnoitre in spite of contrary winds. One of them succeeded in making a tour around Jersey without seeing one enemy vessel, which at least proved that no reinforcements had as yet arrived from England. Another left with orders to land on the island at whatever cost and to bring someone back; there was also talk of sending someone to parley. If he returned to Granville, one would know what he had seen; if he did not it would be that he had been taken and that the island was in British hands and steps could be taken accordingly. The feeling grew that it was time to do something. As de Rullecourt was perhaps master of part of the island it was decided that if a sufficient regular detachment was sent the conquest could be completed.

Since 9 January the Marquis de Ségur had given orders to the Intendant at Caen to make the necessary preparations for a corps of 1,000 men, whom the king had decided to send to Jersey, to embark 'from Granville if this port can make the necessary arrangements for their crossing, and if not, from St. Malo'. A second letter added that a Commissaire de Guerre must accompany them, including 'a division of staff and surgeons for the hospitals'. Similar instructions were sent on the same day to M. de la Bove, Intendant of Brittany. All the necessary preparations were being made at Granville, where there were already sufficient munitions, artillery officers and sappers (whose numbers could be increased if required by M. de Caux, Director General of Sappers, and M. de Riville, Director of Artillery). The town would supply bread, and provisions were collected to last for six weeks. This expedition was to be commanded by M. de la Rosière, Commandant at St. Malo, who was full of optimism about the success of it. He wrote thus to the Minister, thanking him for choosing him (de la Rosière) for the position, and said 'whatever is the fate of this officer [de Rullecourt] everything is ready here to go to his aid, whether it be to support his success, or to protect his retreat, if this is still possible'.

On the orders of the Sub-Delegate at Coutances, 40 sacks of flour were sent to Granville to provision the landing corps. In fact, Guillot, the Commissaire of the Navy, who 'day and night, before and during this event, thought of nothing but what concerned Jersey', took all useful measures for the embarkation of the relief column. He had food and water brought on board the king's vessels, and through his direction, and that of Captain Obet, 28 flat landing craft, 'well caulked, well equipped with rudder, oars, etc.', were waiting to put to sea.

Without delay he left with M. de la Rosière to go by carriage to Granville to join the Duc d'Harcourt and to arrange with him the last details.

The latter, for his part, was in active correspondence with the Minister of War, as is shown in a letter from Guillot to the Ministry. To this was added a list of the conditions of the king's vessels and merchant ships which were near to St. Malo, which could transport 3,000 men, and Guillot had put 21,750 supplementary rations on board. He remarked that it was most opportune to send the expedition, because at the time of the Prince of Nassau's attempt the English had taken 13 days to unite their fleet and to sail towards Cancale; and now only six days had elapsed since de Rullecourt's attack. He enumerated all the artillery that M. de la Rosière had at his disposal, also the 3,000 men, plus the 250 volunteers, who were billeted and out of work at Chausey, and the 200 soldiers of the Nassau Legion. So, considering that the conquest of Jersey and even of Guernsey and Alderney was imminent, d'Harcourt considered what he would do with these islands. His view was that they must not be kept, but only that they should be put in such a condition that they could not harm France, made to pay all the costs of the campaign, and stipulate in the peace which would follow that they would remain for always disarmed.

In the port at Granville merchant vessels—the *Lihou, l'Amitié,* the *Hercules* and *Jean Joseph*—were being armed so that they could participate in the enterprise. Each one of them had to transport 200 men from the 800 soldiers of Berwick's regiment, plus the 200 who had been brought from the Auvergne regiment. But the expedition, so well prepared for the conquest which appeared to be so imminent and so easy, was destined never to embark. The Nassau soldiers concerned were old volunteers of the legion formed by the Prince. They belonged to the Regiment of Nassau Siegen, garrisoned at St. Malo under the orders of Lieutenant-Colonel Diame, who was commanding them in place of the Prince of Nassau, the titular Colonel of the corps.

In Paris, people began to believe in the success of de Rullecourt, who 'by the conquest of Jersey has acquired great honour and an unusual reputation of ability', and they were rejoicing that since 6 January the French flag had been flying in St. Helier; but uncomfortable rumours began to spread during the evening of the 14th. It was reported, without details, that de Rullecourt and all his troops had been made prisoner, and the Marquis de Ségur, when warning the Duc d'Harcourt of these rumours, added that if they were confirmed it would be useless to continue with the arrangements that had been made to help the Baron. Then other contradictory news arrived and was announced in the newspapers. Some said that de Rullecourt had been obliged to re-embark after being beaten; others that he had devastated the island.

Enthusiasm quickly abated. At Court there was no further talk of an important expedition, as the castles and forts in Jersey had not, as they had hoped, been taken. If the king's first intentions were adhered to, de la Rosière would take to

Jersey no more than 1,000 men and eight field guns; then to the great disappoint-
ment of the officers who were to comprise the detachment an order came to
unload the provisions that had been put on the boats. De la Rosière said: 'It is
with real sorrow that I see my hopes for a negative reply from the Court smashed;
all my comrades are as distressed as I; their several dispositions were as well
arranged as the general plan and we should all have embarked on the evening
of the 19th'. During the night of the 17th a courier sent by the Naval Minister,
the Marquis de Castries, to Granville told d'Harcourt of the new arrangements.
At the same time the Minister sent word that 'the Baron de Rullecourt is in
England with the remnants of his army, and that he was only master of the town
until the 7th, having been forced to surrender after a very vigorous defence'.

Meanwhile Major Corbet and the island authorities did not care to have these
tiresome and costly prisoners remaining for long in the neighbourhood, men
who at any moment might have rebelled. At first they though of getting rid of
them in a swift manner by treating the men as filibusters, outside the law of any
civilised country, but this was not possible as Letters of Marque with authority
to undertake the expedition were found among de Rullecourt's papers. It was
decided to send them to England, and already on 9 January the first convoy of
prisoners left St. Helier's parish church, the officers leaving the rooms of the
Royal Court building, under strong escort. This convoy was soon followed by
another on the 15th comprising two captains, two lieutenants, one sergeant-major,
seven sergeants, four corporals, two drummers and 94 privates. A sergeant-major,
one of the drummers, and nine men who still had their equipment, weapons and
18 rounds in their cartridge pouches, were captured later in the Jersey countryside. They miserably gave themselves up to the fisherman Ferdinand Austin
(Aubin?) who passed them over to Captain Campbell. On 11 February six officers
and 150 men disembarked at Portsmouth, and it is said that this brought the
number of legionary officers and soldiers to 500; they arrived in England at
Portsmouth, Plymouth, Falmouth, and in various ports on the Cornish coast.
Only the wounded whose condition was too bad for them to be moved remained
in Jersey, with Major Piatte, a surgeon of the Luxembourg Legion, to care
for them.

The captivity of the officers did not last for long; they were soon exchanged,
as was the usual custom at this period, and sent back to France. Already on the
following 4 March five of them 'returned from England' and signed, at Granville,
the certificate which Régnier had demanded to justify his absence at the time
of the embarkation for Jersey. The soldiers, however, were kept for a year on
pontoons, or prison ships, and it was only in April 1782 that they began to
return to the Continent.

On the 9th of this month the Count de Blangy, Commandant of Middle
Normandy, was in Caen when he received news from General Dumouriez that 252
of the Legion of Luxembourg had just arrived at Cherbourg on an English
packet. This news does not seem to have delighted him, and the letters which

he wrote to the Minister of the Navy and at the same time to the Duc d'Harcourt show both his ill humour and the embarrassment which he felt. 'As the town of Caen is full of troops and foreigners which the fair held here attracts from all sides, I have decided to shut up all these honest men in the chateau'. He added that he was moving the gunners who were there already in order to 'lodge all these gentlemen as well as I can, otherwise I cannot be responsible'.

It had been agreed that when the volunteers returned they would be sent back to the Prince of Luxembourg, who would dispose of them as he pleased; but there were so many of them, far more than had been anticipated, that de Blangy hesitated to send them back to Paris. More than five hundred militiamen from provincial regiments were enrolled in the Legion; it was not likely that the Minister meant to pass them all to the Prince of Luxembourg, particularly as they were experienced in warfare and well fitted for service in the colonies. De Blangy proposed to send them to Brest to complete the crews of ships, and indeed this was also the Prince of Luxembourg's advice. He was no longer in a position to use these men who had returned from England, and he wished, as had the Prince of Nassau, to see them in the king's service. In order to reassure the Governor of Normandy about the costs already incurred, he promised to pay for everything connected with his legion, but he said that the expenses incurred in the expedition to Jersey had been so much multiplied and were at the same time so hard to understand that he had not yet been able to obtain accurate accounts, and that he needed some time to sort this out. This assurance did not prevent M. de Blangy from reducing the costs of transit for these volunteers to the minimum. They were from 20 to 25 sous per day from Cherbourg to Bayeux—where they arrived on the 12th—but Despieds, War Commissioner for Bayeux, reduced it to 8 sous for the future. It may be mentioned here that as one of the men escaped during the journey, further economy was effected.

However, it must not be supposed that their treatment was inhuman. As soon as they arrived at Bayeux the Commissioner had them examined; their condition was deplorable and some had to be sent to hospital. The others were billeted in the Cordeliers' church, which was graciously offered by the Superior. They were enclosed under one roof and they could exercise themselves within a large enclosure surrounded by walls. As their previous stay was well remembered, precautions concerning them were not neglected. A guard of 15 dragoons kept them locked up and not one of them could escape. Each man had a mattress, a blanket and a pair of sheets, and it may be that they had never been so comfortable. Their clothes were in rags and so they were dressed as well as might be in such uniform as could be found in the shops.

The next day an order from the Court at Versailles arrived outlining their future route. It said that they had to go to Fougères, passing through Villiers, Vire, Mortain and St. Hilaire de Harcourt. From there they were to be sent to l'Ile de Ré, a collection point for men destined for the navy. Thus the Legion left Bayeux on the 21st in small groups surrounded by detachments of regular soldiers. On the 29th 96 soldiers, bound for Rennes, passed through Vire, escorted by 26 grenadiers of the regular army. The Sub-Delegate, M. de Mortreux, treated them as criminals and made them sleep in the prison. Their need was so great that he said to M. de Laubarède, 'the officers in command have told me to give shoes to most of the men, who stood in the greatest need of them. I had 40 pairs delivered to them, which at 4 livres 6 sous each comes to 170 livres'. The group which followed was no better off; on 5 May Count de Blangy had 158 shirts and 147 hats delivered to the soldiers from Mantes; the following 25 September it was again necessary to provide shirts, hats and shoes, as they left Bayeux without shirts, and barefoot, with their heads covered only with torn handkerchiefs, having been sent from England thus. All this represented an expenditure of 1,075 livres. But let us leave these unfortunate beings, marching painfully towards a new phase in their uncertain lives, and return to the rear guard, left temporarily on the Grand Ile at Chausey.

Major d'Herville and his troops had scarcely left Granville where they were sent 'no one knowing how or why these men had not followed the rest in landing at Jersey', when it seemed as if they would return there. The Duc d'Harcourt wrote: 'If these troops land at Granville we must, of course, receive them and take steps to find lodging for them. Should they stay for any length of time in your town, I enjoin you, in conjunction with the Commander of the Berwick Regiment, to take the most stringent precautions to maintain them under the strictest discipline, and to prevent them from upsetting public order and tranquillity. You know that with these billets nothing need be provided that is not paid for'. On the same day he told the Minister of War of his fears. He wrote to the Marquis of Ségur that he had given orders to billet them temporarily, as this was unavoidable, but that he hoped to be relieved of these soldiers as soon as possible. Their presence was more than the inhabitants could assimilate, as there were already two battalions of the Berwick Regiment garrisoned in the town.

It was at this point that the Duc d'Harcourt came to Granville to supervise for himself the preparations for the embarkation of the relief column which was to go to Jersey. He was worried about the presence of these volunteers at Chausey, because the island being five leagues from the mainland, was not protected, and the troops could easily be removed by the British if they came with two frigates.It seemed as if the officers knew little about the country and less about their own duties. The first thing that the Governor of Normandy did when he arrived at the coast was to give orders that these men should return to the mainland.

They arrived in a pitiable condition, crawling with lice, and weakened by lack of food and the low temperatures of that season. Yset, the Mayor of the town, could not avoid telling the Intendant of all the measures he had taken: 'If it was a crime on the part of the rear guard Luxembourg Legion not to have succeeded in landing in Jersey, I can assure you that they have redeemed themselves during their stay at Chausey, during the eight days until this afternoon when they returned. I obeyed Mons. the Duc d'Harcourt's orders in billeting them at Hacqueville, a village a quarter of a league from Granville, in quarters situated close together'. On the requisition of the Commissaire de Classes for the sick they were given the childrens' workroom at the hospital. In correspondence from the administrator and directors of the hospital, one learns that their resources were totally insufficient, and that the children had to sleep six in one bed. In addition, to alleviate the total lack of money, a lace-manufacturing system had been established in which children of six or seven worked for their living until they were 11, when they were sent to serve in the navy as ships' boys. Ryan, the Commander of the Berwick Regiment, approved of these arrangements, as he did not want these men to mix with his soldiers. 'The unfortunate men are well advised to accept the care of the Superior, who is full of zeal, and it will not cost our hospital anything, the navy supplying the beds and everything else necessary and undertaking to pay 16 sous per man'.

All these arrangements were ratified by Esmangard, who replied that it was essential that these troops did not have any contact with the garrison, 'and as the navy is responsible for providing for these volunteers, the separation that you have arranged is most useful for the maintenance of order and in order to prevent any sort of confusion'. However, these plans were only temporary, because it was expected that the men would soon be leaving for Jersey. When the expedition was definitely abandoned there was no further reason to keep the men in the town, and means had to be found to disperse them, although no one wanted to leave them to roam the countryside, for fear of their behaviour. So on 17 January they were sent to Dol de Bretagne, the only fortified town in the district. The only remaining soldiers were those from the provincial regiments, who were recalled to the king's service and who were destined to be recruited in the fleet.

The volunteers did not have to stay long at Dol as the Prince of Luxembourg sent them to join the remainder of his legion at the Ile de Ré. These men went on journeys arranged by the Prince or some of his officers, and they behaved everywhere as if they were regular soldiers, demanding lodgings and food from the inhabitants when they arrived at a halting-place. Their demands became so great that the Minister of War had to intervene. He told the Intendant that it was His Majesty's intention that none of his subjects should have to undertake this duty, and he enjoined him to give immediate and precise orders that lodging shall be provided only by paying by mutual agreement.

Men from the Paris and Mantes Regiments, 112 in number, were still at Granville awaiting orders from the Court. They were in a terrible condition; most of them were without under-clothes, as they had been for three weeks or a month, and many were ill. Collet, who was Commissaire of War and who the Duc d'Harcourt had put in charge of policing and disciplining this detachment, claimed a refund for their expenses from the Intendant. At the same time, in order to provide lodgings for these men, the Sub-Delegate at Coutances received an order to distribute 50 beds which he thought could be spared from any parish and to send them to the town hall at Granville. Until this arrangement came into force they were distributed among various houses in the town.

All this caused considerable discontent among the Granville population, who thought with some justification that they were being made to pay rather too much of the country's expenses. Yset, who had shown himself to be most zealous during all these events, was forced to alleviate as far as possible the charges which weighed down upon his people. He said that in order to find lodging for 101 men (bearing in mind that others were receiving treatment at the hospital), he had to evict about seventy inhabitants; with M. Collet he had taken André Besson's house and two others at Le Roc which were empty, and they had to be supplied with the beds referred to above. He added that these men had no leader, that but an officer and several under-officers from the Berwick Regiment were assisting them until orders arrived for their departure, which he hoped would be as soon as possible.

A few days later, on 26 January, these eagerly awaited orders arrived from the Intendant of the Généralité. The instructions from the Court said that the soldiers of the provincial regiments were to leave Granville on 5 February, and to arrive at Villedieu the same day. They were to proceed on the 6th to Cuves, on the 7th to Mortain, and rejoin other troops at Domfront on the 8th; 12 recruits who had come out of hospital at Caen were also to leave. Of those in the Legion of Luxembourg which had gone to Jersey and the provincial detachment, many men were left behind. Those who were ill were dispersed in the hospitals at Caen, Bayeux, Coutances, Avranches, Mortain and Villedieu as well as at Granville and Vire.

The Baron de Rullecourt had died in the market place at St. Helier, the victim of his own rash but intrepid escapade, leaving the impression that he was a rather extraordinary adventurer, who, in a republic, and if he had ended as he had begun, could have been compared with some Romans who are still admired. The volunteers of the Legion of Luxembourg, that is to say those who had survived the enemy shot and bayonet, the sea and illness, trudged on, in misery, on the French roads. Seamen of Granville and St. Malo continued their ordinary life, privateering or fishing, after having repaired their damaged boats, but this damage consisted of no more than some anchors being lost on the reefs at La Rocque or Chausey, torn sails, damaged ropes and hawsers, and oars which were lost or had drifted away.

Through being over-zealous, Lieutenant Ganne (either on orders from Baron de Rullecourt or on his own account), had endeavoured to land his troops on reefs on the Jersey coast, where his lugger was smashed, leaving him eventually in the hands of his enemy, and he was not able to take up his position on the *Pilote des Indes*. Soon after his departure from Granville he was replaced by a relative of Captain Le Tourneur, François Ponée, the lieutenant of a frigate. The

Grenadier who had his leg blown off by the cannon from Elizabeth Castle was able to return home and was given a pension by the king. Everything seems to have ended, and one might hope, at Granville at least, that the attempt on Jersey had become no more than a rather tiresome memory which was best forgotten. It was thus for several months, until demands appeared.

The Prince of Luxembourg, in spite of his good intentions did not know of all the expense caused by the stay of his volunteers in Normandy. The widow of Jacques Fretel, a sailor from Granville, sent a request to the Minister for the Navy at the beginning of 1783; and when forwarding the widow's request to M. de la Porte, Intendant-General of the Navy, Mistral, the Controller in Normandy, explained on 12 February 1785: 'It is clear that the Authorities seized the widow's room, that she and her daughter were obliged to leave, that the few bits of furniture which she had were broken, and that this room was used as de Rullecourt's Paymaster's office for the expedition for six weeks'. The payment for the rent of this room was supposed to have been made out of the funds that Le Chevalier de Luxembourg had for this expedition, but it was never paid even though the amount was small and 40 or 50 livres would have satisfied the widow. She was truly in a miserable situation as her husband was killed in action in the war of 1755. The Marquis de Castries was not deaf to this appeal, and although this payment in no way concerned the navy he had 150 livres paid to Mme. Fretel to indemnify her.

The Destouches brothers made a different sort of demand. Since the attempt on Jersey, these brothers and Jean Orange had lost two shallops on the rocks at Chausey, and they estimated their loss of about five hundred livres. During January 1783 they claimed a reimbursement for this and for 12 sacks of bread which had been provided for de Rullecourt. It seems as if Mistral did not at first accept their demands; because of information that he collected he wrote to M. de la Porte, saying, 'It seems that these shallops and these sacks were not used or lost in this expedition, but to take bread, under orders from Duc d'Harcourt to a detachment of troops which were stationed at Chausey, after the defeat of Mons. de Rullecourt, whether through cunning or otherwise is not known. I am also assured that one of these shallops was worth 200 livres and the other 100, and each sack of bread 5 livres. One must believe this completely as it is no longer possible to make an estimate of them'. Mistral asked himself (without arriving at a conclusion) whether this expenditure, which in any case did not concern the navy, should be charged to the Prince of Luxembourg or to the War Minister.

Finally, on 26 April, François Lalande, a merchant of Granville, asked for 62 livres for having mended 44 mattresses on which the sick of the Legion slept when they returned to France. And so ends an account of the incident which, by world standards, was but a skirmish, but which for Jersey looms as one of the most important dates in island history. It was the last of many attempts by France to conquer an island so close to her shores that it was bound to be a considerable menace in times of hostility between her and Britain.

It was a day when we Jerseymen demonstrated in a practical manner that 'though our language is French our swords and hearts are English'. The Battle of Jersey, renowned in the island where it took place and largely unknown elsewhere, was fought on 6 January 1781, just two centuries ago. Ever since the separation from Normandy, when King John lost that province, France had coveted the group of islands lying so tantalisingly close to her shores, in Victor Hugo's well-known phrase

> '. . . tombés dans la mer
> et ramassées par l'Angleterre'.

This was most understandable: the islands of Jersey and Alderney, in particular, are clearly visible from French shores and in enemy hands constituted a constant danger to shipping and commerce. Their embarrassment to France was in direct proportion to their value to England. And so, inevitably, efforts were made over the centuries to remove this thorn in the flesh of France, and attacks were frequent and often violent and brutal, particularly during the 13th and 14th centuries. None was successful in gaining a permanent foothold, bar the period from 1462 to 1468. The attack of 1781 was the most determined and also the last of these expeditions.

The fact that it failed, largely through the courage of Francis Peirson, and the short duration of hostilities and modest number of casualties should not blind anyone to the potential danger in which the island stood and the ultimate loss for England which it constituted. The preceding pages have shown very clearly that had the scales been tipped in the other direction, the full weight of support would have been forthcoming from King Louis and his army. As it failed it was easy for officialdom virtually to deny knowledge of the expedition, although the many plans put forward and the opinions of senior officers show that the project was being most seriously considered by many people. It is interesting to see the degree of importance our little island held across the 20 miles of sea that separate us from France.

COPLEY'S PICTURE 'THE DEATH OF MAJOR FRANCIS PEIRSON'

John Singleton Copley (1738–1815), who was probably born in Boston, North America, was a Royalist American studying art in Italy; he arrived in London in 1775 and had his studio at 25 George Street, Hanover Square. In 1777 he became an Associate of the Royal Academy and in 1783 the king sanctioned his election as a Royal Academician.

'The Death of Major Francis Peirson' was commissioned by Alderman Boydell of Cheapside, a printseller, who became Lord Mayor in 1790. The picture was completed in 1784 and Boydell proposed that an engraving be made by James Heath. This was done, and was issued to subscribers in May 1796 and sold to non-subscribers in July the same year at a price of four guineas. Heath was the designer of a number of battle pieces for the *Martial achievements of Great Britain and her Allies 1799–1815*; this book contained 50 coloured prints, and Sutherland, the famous aquatinter, engraved them.

Long afterwards, when Boydell's gallery was dispersed, Copley bought back his painting. It was a splendid representation of the action in the Market Place of St. Helier, but there is no evidence that Copley visited Jersey. The woman depicted with a child in her arms was the American nurse of the Copley family, and the woman between her and the wall is Copley's wife, Susannah Clark, the daughter of a rich Boston merchant. The boy is young Copley, who later became Lord Lyndhurst, and was three times Lord Chancellor of England.

Seen in the central group are mainly officers of the 95th Regiment of Foot, and from left to right are Captain David Clephane, Captain Malcolm McNeil, Major Peirson's black servant Pompey, Captain James Corbet (son of the Lieutenant-Governor of Jersey), who was in the 95th, Lieutenant Symeon or Simon Drysdale, Ensign Charles Rowan, Ensign John Smith, Captain Clement Hemery (Royal Jersey Artillery), and Lieutenant Alexander Buchanan. Adjutant James Harrison is supporting Major Peirson, who has just been shot. David Patriarche's house is on the right. Behind the cannon (taken from the parish church) one can see the Court House, and under the royal arms is the door where de Rullecourt was mortally wounded. French troops are wearing a creamy white uniform. King George II's statue (erected in 1751) is not depicted quite correctly, and Captain Hemery was not in uniform on that day. Grenadiers of the 95th are attacking from the left of the painting, and a dying officer of the

78th (Seaforth Highlanders) is shown under the cannon's barrel, although on that day no officer of the latter regiment was wounded. To the top left of the painting, on the heights of Mont de la Ville (now Fort Regent), a section of the 78th Regiment and units of Jersey Militia are seen firing down into the Market Place.

Copley's last work was a portrait of his son, Lord Lyndhurst, which was painted in 1814. He died, aged 78, in London on 9 September 1815.

Military historians consider that 'The Death of Major Peirson' very accurately portrays British army uniforms of the period. The painting was bought by the nation for 1,600 guineas in 1864, and until 1929 was in the National Gallery; it was then placed in the Tate Gallery. It is 8ft. high and 11ft. 11ins. wide.

Other engravings of the death of Major Peirson are those by Kesseler (dated 1800) and Le Breton. The copy of Copley's painting which hangs in the Royal Court of Jersey was painted by William Holyoake (1834–1894), and was bought by the island for £250 in 1866. Further illustrations of the scene are a painting by Burney, an engraving by Springsgarth (published by R. Evans, London, 1815), and an engraving by Thomas Kelly of London.

It is rather surprising to learn that Copley's much-respected painting was actually offered as the first prize in a raffle or lottery organised by John Boydell with the permission of parliament in April 1804. He and his nephew, who was his partner, disposed of their collection of paintings, drawings and engravings together with their leasehold premises in Pall Mall called the 'Shakespeare Gallery'. Twenty-two thousand tickets were to be issued at what must then have been the very high price of three guineas a ticket. The capital prizes were 62, each being a work of art, and every purchaser of a lottery ticket was to receive a print to the value of one guinea.

APPENDIX II

Until October 1834 Jersey's monetary system was to say the least complicated. The money used was issued by the mint of the French city of Tours until 1722 when it ceased operation, although the coinage known as Tournois continued to circulate. Throughout the ages, of course, its value fluctuated, but in the period we are concerned with (i.e., 1781) the 'livre Tournois' was worth sevenpence-halfpenny, or 3p. There were 20 sols to the livre and 12 deniers to the sol. Tournois coins were worth a little less than those of the Paris mint. To complicate matters further there were four coins to the sol known as 'liards', and these were the most common. A gold louis was equal to 24 livres de France in 1809.

APPENDIX III

JERSEY MILITIA OFFICERS, 1781

Rank	Name	Regiment	Date of Commission
Colonels . . .	John Thos. Durell	St. Helier's Battalion[1]	7 July 1770
	Thos. Pipon	South West Regiment	18 May 1771
	Chas. Wm. Lemprière	North Regiment	8 June 1771
	Philippe de Carteret	North West Regiment	1 September 1771
	George Benest	St. Lawrence Battalion[1]	24 July 1773
	Nicholas Messervy	East Regiment	23 May 1778
Lieutenant-Colonels .	Jas Pipon	South West Regiment	18 May 1771
	Math Gosset	St. Lawrence Battalion	17 August 1779
Majors . . .	Thos Hilgrove	St. Helier's Battalion	7 July 1770
	Jas Pipon	North West Regiment	18 October 1770
	Ph. Robin	South West Regiment	18 May 1771
	Edw. Remon	North Regiment	4 June 1774
	John Poingdestre	East Regiment	17 June 1778
	Francis Ricard	North West Regiment	17 September 1778
	Phil Marett	St. Lawrence Battalion	

(South West Regiment Order Book, 1780)

APPENDIX IV

Captain George Charleton, the Commanding Officer of the Invalids, was taken prisoner on the morning of 6 January and was eventually confined to his house by de Rullecourt. Charleton magnanimously invited several French officers to breakfast with him because he pitied them for having to eat black bread. On their departure he was observing events from the window of his house, which was opposite the Court House, and just when he saw de Rullecourt and Corbet emerge his window was shattered by a musket ball and his face was badly wounded by glass splinters.

[1]On Monday, 31 August 1789 Major George Charleton, his son and wife[2] arrived in Jersey from Plymouth. The Major, who for a long time had lived in Jersey, had been recalled to Plymouth where he was taken ill about three weeks previously. He died in Jersey on the following day.

LETTER FOUND AMONG de RULLECOURT'S EFFECTS
(now in the possession of the Author)

To: Monsieur le Baron de Rullecourt,
  Colonel Commandant of the Volunteers of Luxembourg.

Dear Baron,

I could not be more pained on account of the unpleasant things that people have been saying to you about me, which I do not in any way deserve. It is most painful to me to find that they have sought to do me this dis-service at a time when my only aim is to find ways in which to show you my devotion.

The desire that I have to serve under your command has not permitted me to consider what rank you will accord me in the corps under your command, although I have been a serving soldier since 1763, that is to say for 17 years.

As to the letter which Mons. Montardat[1] is asked for on your behalf, if I were about to be guillotined, I could not let you have it, having failed to find it, in spite of diligent searches, since you came away from Mons. d'Aubry's[1] house. I am even tempted to suspect that someone is withholding it in order to make it impossible for me to give you satisfaction in the matter.

I am and always have been prepared to be stationed in the Citadelle, and if I did otherwise it was only after receiving your permission to make arrangements about my private affairs, which will be completed in a few days, as you have mentioned.

I therefore pray you, Mons. Le Baron, to render to me the justice which is due to me and to believe that there is nothing I desire more than to do as you wish, and to give you proof of my zeal, and with these sentiments I have the honour to sign myself

> Your very humble and obedient
>   servant

> Ph de St. Sauveur. I hope that you
>   will let me have a word of reply.

Mons Le Baron
17.7.1780

(Le Chevalier de Saint-Sauveur (Lieutenant) was taken prisoner at the battle)

APPENDIX   VI

A trunk belonging to Baron de Rullecourt was brought to Moses Corbet's house after the battle. The translated inventory[1] is given below:

4 man's shirts	2 pairs of underpants
9 boy's shirts	1 pair of boots
2 dressing gowns	1 pair of shoes
3 towels	1 white bonnet, braided
6 collars	1 silk bonnet with attachments
4 pairs of slippers	1 black cotton bonnet with attachments
6 pairs of silk hose	1 linen bonnet
1 pair cotton hose	1 pair of garters
6 pairs of children's hose	2 silk handkerchiefs
1 overcoat	several pieces of velvet
4 uniforms	5 tassels for swords or canes
2 waistcoats	a pair of gloves
1 cotton waistcoat	7 cards of gold-plated buttons
1 waistcoat ornamented with lace	2 cards of silver braided buttons
5 pairs of long boots	1 piece of gold braid
1 pair of servant's boots	a gold sword tassel (knot)
1 smock or servant's overall	1 jar of snuff
1 pair of half gaiters	

At Dr. Philippe Lerrier's house, where de Rullecourt was taken and where he died from his wounds, his personal effects were:

1 gold-braided blue uniform	1 sword belt and scabbard (the sword he lost before being brought to Lerrier's house)
1 scarlet waistcoat decorated with gold braid	
1 leather high boot	a pair of boots, one of which had been removed from his leg (so that his injuries might be attended to?)
1 gold snuff box, and another with portrait (now in Jersey Museum).	
1 little embossed silver box	St. Jean, his servant, took his shirt, stockings, handkerchiefs and small change

From the possessions he brought with him de Rullecourt obviously intended to stay in Jersey for some time. The boy's shirts and children's hose may have been presents brought on his journey through France for his own children. This huge trunk must have been manhandled all the way from La Rocque, probably by perspiring and cursing soldiers, over the slippery stones and rocks of the Banc de Vielet to the Court House in the Market Place, as there is no evidence of the use of any wheeled transport during the march.

Among the many papers found in de Rullecourt's possession is a receipt for 300 cockades supplied to the Baron as Colonel of the Volunteers of Luxembourg from Bazin of Dunquerque, dated 16 (month illegible) 1780.

There is also an estimate of the value of shipping and effects belonging to the merchants of Jersey amounting to two million livres, and a great number of commissions with blank spaces left for de Rullecourt to sign, in order to fill various civil and military posts. There are also several letters from Régnier, plus maps and descriptions of the island, and an account of the 600 livres given to an engineer, who in November 1780 had made drawings and observations on Jersey's fortifications, military strength and discipline.

After hostilities ceased Madame de Rullecourt visited Jersey to see where her husband was buried; she interviewed all those who gave assistance to her husband during his last moments and gave presents to several of them. She took with her her husband's belongings.

In the Channel Islands exhibition held in 1871 souvenirs of the battle were loaned as follows:

Painting of the 'Battle of Jersey' by local artist Philippe Jean[3] and de Rullecourt's sword loaned by Durell Lerrier, the Lieutenant-Bailiff.
De Rullecourt's dagger (*recte* that of Emir Said?)—Mr. Bichard.
De Rullecourt's bonbonnière—Mr. de la Taste.
De Rullecourt's snuffbox—Mrs. Hugh Godfray.
Ring containing Peirson's hair—Mrs. Hugh Godfray.
Musket taken from a French soldier—Mr. A. A. Le Gros.
Officer's coat worn at the battle—Mr. Dallain .
Portrait of Major Corbet by Philippe Jean—Mrs. Henry Luce Manuel.
De Rullecourt's proclamation and autograph—Mrs. Henry Luce Manuel.

Items presented to La Société Jersiaise Museum were:

De Rullecourt's sword—Mrs. Lerrier, 8 July 1886.
Sword found after the battle—F. de la Taste, 5 April 1894.
Emir Said's 'jamhdar' or dagger—Madame Manuel, 28 March 1896.
Miniature of Peirson by Philippe Jean—Madame Manuel, 8 March 1894.
Gold bonbonnière—by Madame Lerrier, 8 July 1886.
Box holding the above—8 February 1894.
Peirson's watch (unfortunately stolen from the Museum).

Various proclamations issued by de Rullecourt and Corbet can be seen in the Museum Library.

ROUND TOWERS AND/OR GUARDHOUSES

It was thought that the round towers, many of which can still be seen around the islands, were not built until after the French invasion of 1781; however, thanks to the South West Regiment Order Book, which is now in private possession, it can be shown that many were already finished and in use.

These early round towers are wrongly termed martellos, though true martello towers do exist in Jersey. Kempt Tower (1833-36), Lewis (1835), L'Etacq (1834), Portelet (1807-1811), Noirmont (1811-1814), Icho (1811), Victoria (1837), and Point des Pas (1834) are of this pattern. The word martello is a corruption of Cap Mortella in Corsica, where defences from a round tower defeated the attacks of two Royal Navy warships in March 1794. Our early round towers or guardhouses apparently originate from an idea formulated by General Conway, Jersey's Governor, in 1779, probably following the unsuccessful French attack on 1 May of that year. The design and construction of the early towers were under the orders of officers of the Board of Ordnance and Royal Engineers. Captain Basset was succeeded by Captain Frederick George Mulcaster on 14 March 1779 (Société Jersiaise *Bulletin,* 1971).

We need only concern ourselves here with the tower at La Rocque point, No. 1 in Grouville Bay. It is obvious that this tower at La Rocque was in existence in January 1781: 'The arms stores in the towers in Grouville Bay Numbers 1, 2, 3, 4 and 8 being now put in good order and clean . . . 15 hand grenades fixed and 15 empty are immediately to be sent to each of the finished towers' (S.W. Regt. Order Book, 18 October 1779). 'Thursday the 15th of June the Review of the batteries to continue, beginning at St. Clement's guard house at 8 a.m. Platte Rocque at 9 a.m., Tower at 10 a.m., Grouville Bay batteries immediately' (H.Q., S.W. Regt., 30 May 1780).

Jersey towers were 36ft. in height, with a base diameter of 34ft.; the thickness of the walls was 8ft. at the base, decreasing to 6ft. at the crest.

October 1 1780 (*Actes des États*): 'Constable of Grouville to take charge of the middle parapet, Boulevard store and magazine in Grouville Bay. That of St. Saviour's guard house, store and magazine of La Rocque. St. Clement's Store and magazine at La Rocque Platte. Guard house, store and magazine at Rocberg, and accompanying batteries'.

September 1779 (S.J. Library): 'The centinels in the Towers to keep careful watch . . . The men of the 78th at Grouville and also those of the East Regiment (Militia) who may form at any time the tower guards in that bay are to learn the exercise of cohorn (mortar)'.

April 21 1780 (*Actes des États*): 'Constables to supply ½cwt of Bread-biscuit in a barrel and 2 barrels of water to be placed in each of the Towers, 3lbs. of biscuits per man'.

June 18 1781 (*Actes des États*): '. . . where is situated the Tower near le Hocq'.

1779 (S.W. Regt. Order Book): ' A Pattern rack in all guard houses, Bayonets and cartridges boxes are to be hung between the firelocks and should all be numbered with the same number as the firelocks'.

January 1780 (S.W. Regt. Order Book): List of equipment in South Tower, St. Peter (for comparison): 'Arms in good order 8 muskets, 8 Bayonets, 12 cartouches (cartridge) boxes containing 48 cartouches and bullets. 8 Musket flints, 1 screw driver, 1 sand clock, cleaning cloths for the arms, 1 bottle of sweet oil for the arms, emery for the arms, 3 x 24 pound cohorns or mortars. Pile of cannon balls for cohorns, 1 guerite or sentry box' (it will be remembered that Sergeant Falle and his eight men were absent from the tower of La Rocque, eight men being the complement of a tower guard).

1781, letter from Thos. Lemprière (S.J. *Bulletin,* 1904, p. 268): 'The French General possessed a map whereupon all fortifications, towers, cannon etc. were all marked'.

February 12 1781, letter from Thos. Pipon to Lieutenant-Bailiff: 'The chief of the guard of the Tower of La Rocque and eight men were arrested for neglect'.

MS. in S.J. Library: '. . . french landed without being spotted by the guard at La Rocque or Tower No. 2 or Rocqbert (*sic*)'.

January 18 1781, letter from Advocate Lemprière to his father (S.J. *Bulletin,* 1904): '. . . disembarked near La Rocque and passed our guardhouse without being observed, one of the French officers told us that he had slept under the guard house but the guards heard nothing. The guards are now in prison'.

In the Société Jersiaise Library is a booklet entitled 'Hints on the state and fortifications of the bays and landing places in Jersey, June 1778', an interesting notebook written anonymously, but obviously by a military engineer officer, since the book contains firing tables, ranges, and so on. It could possibly have been Captain Frederick Mulcaster or Captain Basset. Among detailed recommendations for positioning towers and other fortifications around the island, the following observations by this officer are particularly relevant:

From the point of the Havre-des-pas to La Motte[1] is 2,666 yards, and from La Motte to a point near La Rocque is about 3,200 yards.

Great part of this is called Grève de St. Clement, behind it and rather to the westward is the plain or strand called vint (*sic*) de Saumares, this is covered all along to the southward by a range of rocks in the sea, which have some openings frequented by the fisher boats and smugglers from France on which account it deserves some attention.

On the eastern side towards La Rocque is a sandy shore called Havre-du-haut opposite to which is an entrance for boats and at the Banc-de-Vielet near La Rocque is another target.

The road from La Rocque towards St. Helier, should a landing be made in Grouville Bay, or near La Rocque is almost everywhere a strong pass and by fortifying some points might stop almost any force that should be brought, particularly near La Motte, a point which commands the roads and sands. Here should be a Tower and battery. Also on the point near Le Havre-du-Haut another Tower and battery on a pointed rock on the land between there is a strong pass which should be occupied.

In that part it seems possible for a number of men to be landed at low water and in still weather at a great distance to march up on the openings between the rocks.

There are also many houses and particularly two large farms with walls where strong posts might occasionally be made.

Grouville Bay. The extent of Grouville bay from the point of La Rocque to Mont Orgeuil Castle is about $2^1/_3$ miles the whole is uniform and flat, the tide ebbing at spring tides yards from the shore. No ship can come near this shore so as to bear on the defences. A Tower and circular works should be erected at the point of La Rocque, where an old tower stood.

About 6 more Towers from hence along the shore between that and the unfinished Redoubt (Fort Conway?). One Tower between this and the Redoubt called the French Redoubt (Fort William?) and one more near the road between that Redoubt and Orgueil Castle.

In all 9 being in general in all the open ports at about 400 yards apart. The great unfinished Redoubts should have one angle made up as a strong square Tower which may be done for a trifle, the materials are on the spot.

The stone there would contribute very considerably to the other Towers.

February 11 1799, Surveyor General's minutes: 'That Captain Mulcaster proceed upon the works (i.e., towers) contained in Captain Basset's estimate of 22.12.1779 for Jersey . . . that Captain Basset deliver to him, plans and sections of the towers . . . that he be on the same footing at Jersey as Capt. Basset at Guernsey and that they do not interfere with each other' (S.J. *Bulletin,* 1971, p. 290).

The nine negligent guards from tower No. 1 at La Rocque who were tried at the Royal Court on 17 January 1781 were from the East Regiment of Militia and were named as Sergeant Clement Falle (Chef de la Garde), Nicolas Poing-destre, Jean Poingdestre, Clement Laffoley, Charles le Vesconte, Philippe Marett,

Jacques Pirouet, Jacques Bertram, and Philippe Le Noble. Sergeant Falle was imprisoned and the rest were cautioned. The South West Regiment Order Book of 30 May 1780 gives the following important information: 'Inspection of . . . Batteries on the 13th June will continue beginning at St. Clement's guard house at 8 a.m., Platte Rocque at 9 a.m., Tower No. 1 and Grouville batteries immediately afterwards . . .'. This proves that there was a battery at Platte Rocque and that tower No. 1 was already built.

Headquarters, Jersey, 30 December 1780: Paroles or passwords for the day:

January 1—York
    „   2—Athole
    „   3—Leeds
    „   4—Perth
    „   5—Coventry
    „   6—Inverness

THE AFFAIR OF EDOUARD MILLAIS

Edouard Millais, a wealthy farmer and shipowner of 'Le Tapon', St. Saviour, came from an old-established Jersey family. He married Elizabeth Falle in 1752, the daughter of Edward and Elizabeth Anthoine. Millais's children were Edouard, Jean, Abraham, Anne and Jeanne. Edouard first attracted attention when in 1765 he leased one of the smaller islands of Chausey for the harvesting of vraic.[1] He caused difficulties for the tenant of Chausey, Régnier senior, refusing to obey the harvesting rules and inciting other Jerseymen to do likewise. In the first days of July 1768 Millais disembarked at Chausey and menaced workers in the quarries who were cutting stone for the French king. He removed the beams from the castle and burnt the rest after having destroyed Régnier's house.[2]

Eleven years later he must have made up his quarrel with Régnier, as we read in a letter dated 5 February 1779 from Monsieur d'Hericy (King's Commander of Lower Normandy) to the Duc d'Harcourt from Valognes: 'I believe that Mons. Régnier has gone to Jersey under a parliamentary flag. What is more, Mons. de la Rocque (Commander of Granville) informs me that he prepares himself for this voyage and had promised to restore the correspondence from Chausey from taking engagements with Monsieur Millais and taking from him all the information he can extract from this island'.[3]

Papers found on de Rullecourt's body incriminate Millais further, and in letters written by Advocate Lemprière to his father he states that 'Millais is detained in Elizabeth Castle in manacles and leg irons under suspicion of keeping a correspondence with the French and a letter found on the Baron de Rullecourt says that if he needs horses he will get them from Millais, this man is rich and has a large family'.[4] In a further letter we read: 'Edouard Millais is still detained in prison. A seal is placed upon his house, the papers in his mail have been seized, no one is allowed to see him in prison'.

Curiosity drove the author to the Ministry of Defence Library, where he found the following:

Privy Council, 12.6.1781, Vol. 1, p. 389: 'Edouard Millais. Confined on a suspicion of a treasonable correspondence some time since but now enlarged upon bail'.

Later—21.12.1781: 'Advises discharge of Millais' bail'. This was done on 2 February 1782.

So apparently Millais was released through lack of evidence, his 13 months' incarceration having obviously made up for de Rullecourt's incriminating papers.

In 1835 the family moved to Dinan in France; two years later they returned to Jersey and by 1838 they were in London. John Everett Millais, the artist, was born on 8 June 1829, the son of John William and Emily Mary. John William, a quiet country gentleman and an officer in the Jersey Militia, lived at 'La Coie House' until he moved to Southampton. Philippe Raoul Lemprière of Rozel Manor was a friend of the artist, and General Arthur Lemprière, R.E., grandson of Philippe, was the model for the 'Huguenot' which Millais painted in 1852.

JEAN RÉGNIER

Captain Jean Louis Christophe Régnier (1742–1802) was Concessionnaire of the Chausey Islands (as was his father, who died in 1772). From 10 June 1780 he was Master of the Granville privateer *La Sauterelle,* and he took a large part in the preparations for the invasion of Jersey but did not accompany de Rullecourt. Having sold his concession to the Baron he had been sent to purchase wheel-barrows and stores in Granville to fortify three forts on the Chausey Islands as a forward post for de Rullecourt. Régnier knew Jersey and the islanders very well as he was involved with them in the lucrative trade of smuggling.

While de Rullecourt was in Chausey with his forces Régnier and Le Tourneur had constantly cruised between the Islands of Chausey and the coast, keeping a close lookout and reporting to General Dumouriez, the Commander of Cherbourg, who was so pleased with the information he received that on 22 October 1780 he gave Régnier a certificate of recommendation. Régnier wrote in his diary 'that the intention of the Luxembourg Legion was to attack Jersey on Christmas night when the English indulge in the pleasures of the table, and therefore will be most unlikely to defend themselves'. De Rullecourt had promised Régnier 300,000 livres in November 1780 in the name of the Duke of Luxembourg if he (de Rullecourt) disembarked in Jersey.

Régnier was succeeded as Tenant of Chausey by Jacques Pimor of Granville in July 1786. Régnier then lived at Granville and became a constructor of military buildings including Fort Royal and Fort d'Artois at Cherbourg. He was married with several children, and died in 1802 whilst serving in the 6th Half Brigade of Veterans in action in the Ardennes.

(*Les Iles Chausey,* by de Gibon)

APPENDIX X

'La Hougue' in the parish of St. Peter was the barracks for the 95th Regiment in 1781, but it was also the birthplace of Philippe de Carteret (1639-1682) who became the first Governor of New Jersey. Elizabeth de Carteret of La Hougue married Nicholas Fiott in 1758; he was married again in 1772 to Jeanne Remon of St. Lawrence, the lady who was struck by a musket ball during the battle. Nicholas Fiott leased La Hougue for the use of the 95th.

One hundred and sixty-one years later during the Second World War La Hougue became the headquarters of a German anti-aircraft battery. The present house on the same site was built in 1822.[1]

'John Moisson a militiaman of St. Helier who had been slightly wounded in escaping from the French in town, Major Peirson seeing him out of uniform desired him to shut up a favourite dog which had followed him from his residence at St. Peter. The circumstances prevented Mr. Moisson being near Peirson when he fell'.[1]

* * * * *

Regimental Song of the Defence of Jersey

'When staying at a shooting lodge on the Lochcarron Forest in Rossshire in 1895, I came across an old man living in a small croft of my cousin's estate, who told me he was a deserter from the 72nd Highlanders. He came down one evening when I sent for him, and sang the attached song which he informed me was a regimental song that used to be regularly sung in the regiment when he was in it.

'The tune, to which he appeared to attach great importance, was an old Highland air, and I am trying to get it written down. He told me he had deserted when on furlough from Windsor the end of 1841, and said that in those days, owing to there being no police in that part of the Highlands, deserters were rarely ever looked for.

'His name is Donald McDonald and he joined the regiment in the beginning of 1840 being posted to the No. 3 Company (Captain O'Briens). His two grand uncles Donald and Colin Campbell were at the defence of Jersey.

'The song was written by the Bard Counanach or the Strathconan Bard who was himself at the taking of Jersey.'

Aldershot
December 1895

M. D. Murray, Captain of
Seaforth Highlanders

Literal Translation of Song (The Seaforth Defence of Jersey)

> On Christmas Eve in Jersey
> We stood for the honour of the Gael
> We kept the 'top stone of the street' (i.e. the crown of the causeway)
> And we gave fair play to the foe.

The news for which I am saddest now
Is that we have lost our chief adviser
Major Peirson the descendant of heroes
Who never feared an enemy.

The Frenchmen got their share of Christmas fairing
But when they did it was far from agreeable
If I do not err in these verses
There were many hundreds of them lifeless.

Immediately before the break of day
The cannon were incessantly firing
Silken banners fluttering in the breeze
And heroes going forth to the strife.

Shortly before the setting of the sun
Numerous were the brides without spouses
Many the mother whose sons were not to be found
And sisters who had lost a handsome brother.

Many were the fatigues we suffered
Since we donned the red coat
Eager to advance in the face of hardship
And to conquer wherever we went.

Once on the top of Dunedin hill
There was a splendid gathering
Arrayed in kilts and tartan plaids
In the presence of Scotland's Chiefs.

Now I am lying in the low country
Useless and inactive
Gazing out upon the stars
Oh Strathconan! Thou art far West from me.

Translated by Q.M. Sergeant John Mackenzie

Reproduced by permission of Lieutenant-Colonel Angus A. Fairrie, Regimental Headquarters, Queen's Own Highlanders (Seaforth and Camerons), Fort George, Ardersier, Inverness.

APPENDIX XII

Note to all Regiments of Militia:[1]

'The Governor cannot sufficiently express his thanks to the regulars and Militia for their distinguish (*sic*) behaviour this day which he was released and the Country saved, the death of Major Pierson (*sic*) is a serious loss in every sense. He lost his life exerting himself at the head of a set of Brave Men.

'The Garrison of Elizabeth Castle under the command of Capt. Aylward, are equally comprehended and most justly entitled to the same and Capt. Mulcaster repairing to that garrison, so early as he did was a serious assistance to those troops that gave proofs of their intention.'

Moses Corbet, Lt. Governor

*   *   *   *   *

November 5 1881: The three regiments of Militia infantry received authority to inscribe 'Jersey – 1781' upon their colours.

APPENDIX XIII

Thomas Anley (1757-1827). During the period of the battle he was a lieutenant in the St. Helier's battalion of the 4th Regiment. He was in bed when de Rullecourt occupied the town. He dressed, went to the Market Place and questioned some French officers, who told him that they had landed 10,000 men and that all the regulars had surrendered. He heard de Rullecourt bullying Corbet in the Court House into signing the capitulation. Anley then went home to breakfast, and when he heard that the Militia were gathering on Gallows Hill he made his way there by a devious route and offered his services to Major Peirson. As most of Anley's men were trapped in the town Peirson sent him to find a company of the North Regiment of Militia under Officer Thomas Gallichan which had halted at the Town Mills, and to guide it by the back lanes to Gallows Hill. This he did and by his words greatly encouraged the men. Clement Hemery, by then a Major, informs us in the *Gazette de l'Isle de Jersey* of 23 June 1792 that Thomas Anley also carried a message from Major Peirson to the Commanding Officer of the 83rd Regiment.

At Major Corbet's court martial he was a witness for the defence. He had a peculiar appearance, being unusually tall and thin, and his long legs were made to appear even thinner by his habit of wearing very short light trousers. His nickname was Baron de Latte (lath). He was proud of a pigtail of his own hair which he tied with a red rosette. He became Constable of St. Helier and a Jurat of the Royal Court. Anley Street in Jersey is named after him.

Other streets with names linked with the battle are Peirson Road, Peirson Place and Mulcaster Street; the *Peirson* hotel is the building in which Baron de Rullecourt was taken when he was mortally wounded.

Among many islanders who distinguished themselves that day were two brothers of the Robin family, Major Philippe Robin (1738-1821) and Captain Charles Robin (1743-1824) of Newfoundland fisheries fame, both serving in the 5th or south West Regiment of the Jersey Militia.

In the confusion of the battle in or near the Market Place, a gunner was about to ignite the charge of a field-piece which would doubtless have brought down several of our own people, had not Major Robin been luckily at hand. He covered the touch-hole with the tip of his sabre, and at the same time snatched the burning match out of the gunner's hand. (Société Jersiaise *Bulletin*, Vol. II, p. 278.)

Included in these interesting letters from Advocate Thomas Lemprière to his father (as quoted above) is the following statement: 'Peirson fell at my side, a short while after I myself was hit in the shoulder just as the French surrendered'. Lemprière managed to drag himself to the nearby house of Dr. Gosset.

Chevalier de Baudraye, the French officer taken prisoner, was a relation of Madame Lemprière from Port-Bail; he wrote a polite note to Advocate Lemprière enquiring about his wound and wanting to see him before his departure as a prisoner to England. Lemprière had often met him at Valognes in France at the house of the Marquis de Bellfond, his uncle.

Louis François de Macquart, Chevalier of the Order of St. Louis, Seigneur de Soisy, etc., was one aristocrat who fled from France to Jersey to escape the horrors of the French Revolution. He had served as a captain in the Royal Army. He was 10 years younger than his relative the Baron de Rullecourt, who invaded the same island as that in which Macquart himself was to seek hospitality. He died in Jersey in October 1807, and is buried in St. Saviour's parish cemetery. (Société Jersiaise Library, S.B.F. 7.)

APPENDIX XIV

'The events of the sixth of January 1781 stopped abruptly the policy of negligence, half measures and procrastination which had jeopardized Jersey's security for 600 years. The lesson was rammed home. No more chances were taken and long before the Napoleonic era had ended Jersey had become impregnable.'

(Written in the 1920s by Jersey historian Major N. V. L. Rybot, D.S.O.)

*   *   *   *   *

O.K.W. Berlin HQ, June 1940.

Message to all active German units in the area—

THE CAPTURE OF THE BRITISH CHANNEL ISLANDS IS BOTH NECESSARY AND IMPORTANT

NOTES

Chapter I

1. MS. in Société Jersiaise Library. These were the origins of Forts Henry and William.
2. MS. in Société Jersiaise Library.

Chapter II

1. Records suggest this figure is an exaggeration.
2. Dumouriez was wrong about the militia.
3. There is no proof of an actual landing.
4. Dumouriez forgets that the 'few natives' were supported by half of the 78th Regiment of Foot and 2,500 Jersey Militia.

Chapter IV

1. The title of 'Royal' for the Jersey Artillery had been confirmed in Council in 1771, each parish having 1 lieutenant, 1 instructor and 12 gunners, all, as the *Actes des États* state 'composed of the best people'.
2. Pirouet, *Chronique de Jersey* (1788), p. 16.
3. In 1781 the States granted his widow and children £100 cash grant (*Actes des États*).
4. In his account Brachet also states 'Nassau's Second in Command actually landed for a short while and endeavoured to rally his men'.
5. Brachet says 'that she was Marie Felicité de Vissal, daughter of Compte de la Ferté Morteville'.

Chapter V

1. Extract from South West Militia Regimental Order Book, 8 November 1779: 'escaped from prison where he was confined for robbery, a soldier of the 83rd Regiment James Mahon aged 20 of Ireland enlisted with Ensign Brown at Perth in Scotland in the 83rd Regiment on the 6th March 1778 . . . all outgoing boats to be examined'. It is possible that this was the deserter named above. Other deserters from the 83rd Regiment were William Osborn, aged 16, deserted 10 June 1779. and James Smith, deserted 7 July 1779.
2. Jones, John Paul (1747-1792). Born in Scotland, naval officer of the American Revolutionary war; became a midshipman in the British navy. By 1775 he received a commission as senior lieutenant in the new Continental navy.
   In 1777 he sailed for France and there successfully commanded French ships in action against the British. Louis XVI of France presented him with a gold-hilted sword and made him a Chevalier of France. In 1781 he returned to the United States.
3. Money was a great problem for de Rullecourt and among those from whom he borrowed was Pierre Augustin Caron de Beaumarchais (1732-1799), a dramatist, author of the *Marriage of Figaro*, who had other interests as a financier and moneylender (*Les Iles Chausey*, Vicomte de Gibon, Coutances (1918), p. 409).
4. Liverpool Observatory and Tidal Institute. Time of high water on 6 January 1781, 3.45 a.m.; of low water on 6 January 1781, 10.00 a.m.; Range 18ft. The tides were somewhat past neap on 5/6 January 1781.

5. Letter written to the Chevalier de Luxembourg.
6. Now preserved in the Société Jersiaise Museum. De Rullecourt's spelling of names varies considerably.

Chapter VI

1. The present house was built on the site in 1822.
2. In the *Actes des États* (1781), published by the Société Jersiaise there is a footnote saying that he was the younger brother of the Lieutenant-Governor.
3. 'Cabar Feidh' is Gaelic for 'antlers of the deer', the warcry of the Seaforths, also a phrase for clan.

Chapter VII

1. Saunders MS. in Société Jersiaise Library.

Chapter IX

1. *L'Impartial*, 10 July 1844.
2. Saunders MS. in Société Jersiaise Library.
3. *Actes des États*, 1 July 1780.

Chapter X

1. Arrivé's house was sited on what is now a small garden adjoining Snow Hill steps.
2. Gosset's became the *Union* hotel in the Market Place.
3. *L'Histoire de la Bataille de Jersey*, by F. Jeune, p. 17.
4. Jean Cabot was also killed in La Grande Rue (Broad Street). (*La Nouvelle Chronique*, 2 November 1864.)
5. Erected in July 1751, but until 1810 mounted on a different pedestal.
6. *Vide* evidence at the Trial of Moise Corbet.
7. At about 7 a.m. Captain Campbell sent Lieutenant William Nivon to St. Helier for instructions from the Lieutenant-Governor; Nivon was, however, taken prisoner.
8. *Glasgow Mercury*.
9. Société Jersiaise *Bulletin*, 1939.

Chapter XI

1. At this period two militia cannon were kept in each parish church.
2. MSS. at Société Jersiaise Library.
3. 'Lately died in Grouville, aged 92, Jane Noel, widow of Philippe Aubin. In 1781 she accompanied the North Regiment of Militia to La Rocque and fired the last shot at the French invaders. When learning of de Rullecourt's defeat in St. Helier she took off her bonnet threw it in the air giving three hurrahs' (*Le Constitutional*, 5 December 1857).
4. At the trial of Moses Corbet it was stated that Lieutenant William Nivon delivered a capitulation note to Fort Conway at 1 p.m.
5. Further details of this remarkable man are given in G. R. Balleine's *Biographical Dictionary of Jersey*, p. 374.
6. Twelve were accidentally disinterred in 1859.

Chapter XII

1. He survived this terrible wound to be given a pension in France.
2. *An authentic account of the Invasion of Jersey*, printed for C. Le Feuvre, 18 Beresford Street, 1867.

Chapter XIII

1. Some reports say there were casualties.
2. Compiler of the Code of Laws.

3. Now the *Peirson* hotel.
4. Now Gallichan, the jeweller.
5. At the corner of what is now Don Street.
6. Lived at Belle Vue, Mont au Roux (1773-1792).
7. Now Burtons.
8. The actual bullet may be seen in the Jersey Museum.
9. Now the *Peirson* hotel.

Chapter XIV

1. *Almanach de la Chronique* (1872).
2. *La Chronique de Jersey.*
3. Fiott papers, Société Jersiaise Library.
4. Probably Captain Jean Baptiste de Roux, publican, of St. Lawrence. He married a Miss Le
      Cras; died in May 1790.
5. Near Platte Rocque House, La Rocque.
6. A gold louis was equivalent to 24 livres.
7. Société Jersiaise *Bulletin*, 1939, p. 413.

Appendix III

1. The St. Helier and St. Lawrences Battalions combined formed the South Regiment.

Appendix IV

1. *Gazette de l'Isle de Jersey*, 5 September 1789.
2. Delicia, the daughter of Dr. Philippe Lerrier (Payne's *Armorial*).

Appendix V

1. Le Chevalier d.Aubrey and Le Chevalier de Montardat were captains in de Rullecourt's army.

Appendix VI

1. MS. in Société Jersiaise Library.
2. Bonnet was a term then used for a military hat. It seems especially appropriate, as we are
      told that they were ornamented or laced with attachments.
3. Its whereabouts are unknown.

Appendix VII

1. Green island.

Appendix VIII

1. Seaweed to be used as fertiliser.
2. *Les Iles Chausey*, by Gibon, p. 352.
3. *Ibid.*, p. 623.
4. MS. in Société Jersiaise Library.

Appendix X

1. *Old Jersey Houses*, Vol. II, p. 140.

Appendix XI

1. Société Jersiaise Library, Filleul Scrapbook, p. 68.

Appendix XII

1. South West Regiment Order Book.

INDEX

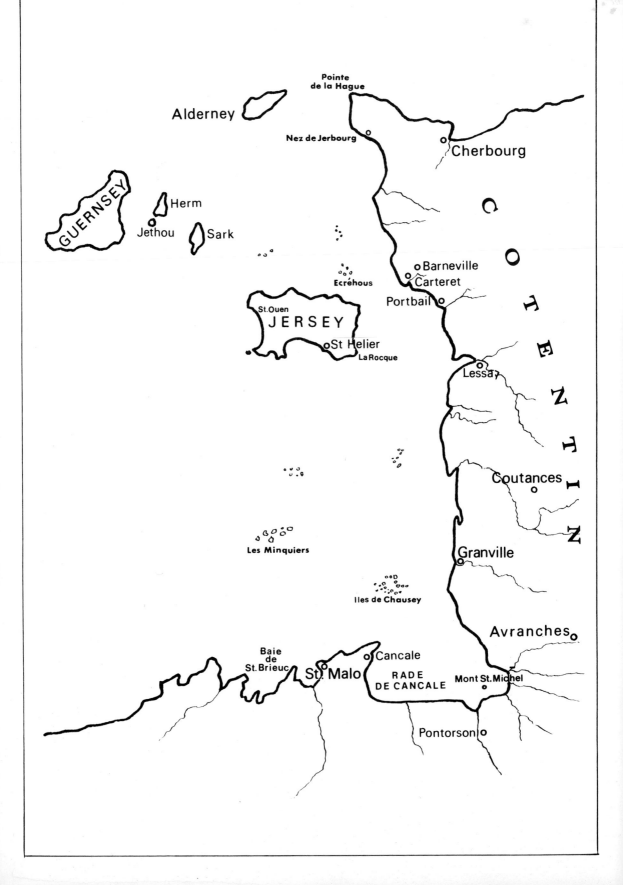